D1176346

Becoming Mama

YVROSE TELFORT ISMAEL

with CRAIG BORLASE

HARVEST HOUSE PUBLISHERS
EUGENE, OREGON

Unless otherwise indicated, all Scripture quotations are taken from The ESV® Bible (The Holy Bible, English Standard Version®), copyright © 2001 by Crossway, a publishing ministry of Good News Publishers. Used by permission. All rights reserved.

Verses marked NLT are taken from the Holy Bible, New Living Translation, copyright © 1996, 2004, 2015 by Tyndale House Foundation. Used by permission of Tyndale House Publishers, Inc., Carol Stream, Illinois 60188. All rights reserved.

Verses marked NIV are taken from the Holy Bible, New International Version®, NIV®. Copyright © 1973, 1978, 1984, 2011 by Biblica, Inc.® Used by permission. All rights reserved worldwide.

Cover design by Connie Gabbert Design + Illustration

Cover photos © Sylvie Corriveau, Mateusz Liberra / Shutterstock

Published in association with the literary agency of D.C. Jacobson & Associates LLC, an Author Management Company. www.dcjacobson.com; Lauren Yono—assistant; lauren@dcjacobson.com

Becoming Mama
Copyright © 2019 by Yvrose Telfort Ismael
Published by Harvest House Publishers
Eugene, Oregon 97408
www.harvesthousepublishers.com

ISBN 978-0-7369-7765-4 (pbk)
ISBN 978-0-7369-7766-1 (eBook)

Library of Congress Cataloging-in-Publication Data is on file at the Library of Congress, Washington, DC.

All rights reserved. No part of this publication may be reproduced, stored in a retrieval system, or transmitted in any form or by any means—electronic, mechanical, digital, photocopy, recording, or any other—except for brief quotations in printed reviews, without the prior permission of the publisher.

Printed in the United States of America

19 20 21 22 23 24 25 26 27 / VP-GL / 10 9 8 7 6 5 4 3 2 1

CONTENTS

Part Four

I want to thank God for transforming my life from a rebel to a servant.

This book is for my husband, Pierre-Richard, for embracing me when I was rejected, for sharing and running the race of life faithfully with me, for being a great father to my children, and for keeping the faith when I am down.

This book is for my mom and dad, who brought me into this world.

This book is for my 38 children, for bringing joy and happiness in my life.

This book is for my brother-in-law, Louis Derosier, who encouraged me and paid my first semester in college.

This book is for Marie Desroses, who taught me how to pray the will of God, how to listen to God, and how to say yes to God's call.

This book is for all my sisters and brothers who encouraged me to stay in school.

This book is for all my friends who have supported me since I returned to Haiti.

This book is for all those who have supported Hope House Haiti.

And this book is for all the churches who served us locally and internationally.

PROLOGUE

Port-au-Prince, Haiti. Tuesday, January 12, 2010. 4:53 p.m.

Breathless, I try to roll from my back to my knees. I get halfway up, but then it happens again. I am thrown into the air. I hang here, just for a beat. Weightless. Then I am hurled down once more onto my back.

Forty-six years I have lived on this earth. Not once has it ever moved beneath my feet. Not once has it ever stirred. But the earth is no longer asleep. The planet is awake—and incensed. It is a violent, raging giant. It wants to be rid of all us parasites that have dared to touch its surface.

Another surge slams me down onto my side. It throws me the way a dog wrestles with a stolen toy, the way a cow's back will spasm to dislodge the flies that have settled upon it.

I spend these first seconds of the earthquake in a state of shock. Nothing makes sense. I wonder what is wrong with my hearing, for my ears have been robbed of all the familiar city sounds that had filled the air moments before. Then I realize that the strange feeling in my ears is not deafness but a noise so loud as to be deafening. The sound of the city being torn apart.

With this new realization comes terror, slamming into me with a force even greater than this concrete trampoline beneath me. I can taste the fear in my mouth, feel it all the way down to my stomach. It tastes like stale blood. *Jesus,* screams the prayer deep within me. *Save us!*

A series of kicks from the ground and I am thrown across the street, tumbling, twisting, dragged through air and rubble by invisible ropes. Only when I come to a halt do I look back at where I was standing—the familiar street corner not far from my mother-in-law's home—and see it disappear under a cloud of bricks and dust. The sound alone is enough to crush me.

The street is narrow, barely wide enough for two cars to pass each other. I look up to see the wall of the building above me bulge and billow, like it is trying to hold back an ocean. It starts to crack and break up, and I know exactly what is about to happen. Another peal of thunder comes from the bricks and I see the wall break away and fall toward me. This is it. This is the moment of my death.

I'm flying.

The earth sends me first to the left, then to the right, a paper bag caught in a hurricane. I hear the earth explode behind me. Everything happens so fast I do not know whether all of this is real or not. Am I really getting pulled out of the way moments before these buildings come down? And why do I feel no pain? Has death already happened?

I open my eyes. I am 20, maybe even 30 feet from where I was when the earthquake started. The street corner has disappeared. Vanished. The buildings that once stood so tall on both sides are now spread out across the road, nothing but bricks and dust and sky.

I breathe. At last the ground is still.

For a while, the air is quiet. A handful of car horns are bleating, but they are weak and feeble after the chaos of the last 30 seconds. And then, as if on the cue of some invisible conductor, the screaming starts up.

"Save us!" some call.

"Jesus! Jesus!" plead others.

Other cries sound more like those of a wounded, terrified animal. No words. Just pain and fear from the lips of men and women, adults and infants. I try to look, but I can't see any of them. The air is misted, a thin cloud of dust that catches in my throat as I try to breathe.

I check my body for cuts and breaks but don't expect to find any. I know that I have been protected, that not a hair on my head has been harmed.

I get to my feet and struggle back toward the corner. A figure approaches, more like a ghost than a man. He's covered in gray dust, and in his arms he carries a child, a little girl who can't be older than five or six. She's also painted gray, but there's blood covering most of her face. Her legs and arms hang limp as they pass by.

For the first time in what feels like forever, I exhale. *I am alive. I am alive. Thank You, Jesus.*

I stand at what's left of the corner, trying but failing, then trying and failing again to reach my husband, Pierre-Richard, on my cell phone. When I finally give up, I notice that the cries have grown louder and a crowd has formed nearby. Some people are helping drag others out of buildings, others can only stand and watch as those who are trapped can barely force an arm out through an impossibly small gap. Bodies lie on the ground; some are alone, others have people beside them, weeping or frantically trying to help.

Why do I get to survive when so many others have not? I push the thought away for now. I cannot stop. I have to get back.

* * * * * * * * * * * *

As soon as I see my mother-in-law's house, I cry. Waves of relief wash over me as I approach the one-story timber and mud home, which is still standing. I step into the front yard. Every-one is alive.

That's when the question returns and ignites within me. *Why me? Why am I alive?*

As sure as the dust in my mouth and eyes, I know that God has heard my question and that He has an answer for me.

"You are alive to do My will. That's why I've put you in this place. You are here to represent Me. That's why you are alive."

The tears come almost instantly. It's like I am a child again, a newborn. I feel weak and vulnerable but also called into life by my loving Father. My every breath is dependent on Him. My life is His. I have felt this way before—years earlier when I was living in Florida and I handed over control of my life to Him. There were no earth-quakes then, but my life was in ruins all the same. And just like He is doing now, God held His arms wide open and bid me come to Him. What had I done to deserve such love and kindness?

For the twentieth time I try to phone Pierre-Richard, but again the call doesn't go through. I have tried so hard not to panic, but as I sit and wait in the house he grew up in, I cannot hold back the fear any longer. I replay the last phone call we had, just five minutes before the earthquake struck.

It had been one of those calls that you have with your husband when you get home from a long trip where you have been apart. There was way too much to say in a simple phone call, so we stuck to the facts about where and when he was going to collect me. We ended the call the way we always do, saying "I love you." Those three words don't seem enough somehow. Why didn't I tell him just how much I love him?

The thought that I might never speak to him again terrifies me. Fear infects every cell in my body. I can taste the blood in my mouth.

．　．　．　．　．　．　．　．　．　．　．　．

The sun was glowing warm red and starting to set when the earthquake struck, but as I sit and pray and hope desperately for Pierre-Richard to arrive, the city slips into darkness. I can feel myself slipping, too, so I try to distract myself by walking the streets looking for people to help. I don't stray far from the house. I'm hoping that Pierre-Richard will return soon.

Even though I am armed with nothing more than water and cotton swabs, I do what I can. It helps quell the fear within for a while.

There's no power, but the streets are alive with light. People are searching frantically with flashlights among the debris, and in places the sky glows orange as fires burn out of control. It's chaos out here, and more than once I flinch at the sound of cars crashing into each other a few feet from where I am working.

I am walking back to the house when I hear shouting coming from it. I run as fast as I can. Fear and hope rise with every step.

I keep on running when I see him. Pierre-Richard looks up, sees me, and falls to the ground. He is alive and unharmed as far as I can tell. The relief I feel is total, as if my body is finally given fresh air to breathe after a month of being locked inside. He's sobbing, and I am, too, as I crouch down beside him on the ground. For the longest time Pierre-Richard can't speak. All he can do is gulp at the air in between sobs.

"It was the bodies, Yvrose," he whispers. "They're all over the street. I had to drive around them. Some of them were…"

He breaks off and cries once more.

We have been married three years, but we have been through enough together to know that some conversations need to be put aside for when there is enough time. Right now, with God's words loud in my head, I take hold of his hands, step back, and fix my eyes on his. "We're alive," I say. "We're alive and there's got to be a reason why. Let's get to work."

We grab some more supplies from his car—a tube of Neosporin, some painkillers, and water—and head out together. In the middle of all this death and fear, I take a moment to thank God for sending me a man of such faith and courage.

We work together, pulling people out of the rubble, sharing our water, tending to broken arms and legs and cleaning wounds as best we can. I am thankful for my years of nursing training in South Carolina as much as I am for the man by my side. I'm thankful, too, for the little tube of Neosporin. Every time I think it's about to run out, there's enough inside to help. It's a miracle—a small one, but a miracle all the same.

We try to move quickly, aware that around every corner there are more people who need help. My training helps me think clearly and fast, keeping my emotions far enough back to be able to work. But from time to time I am truly shocked by what I see, such as the mother frantically asking everyone if they know where her baby has gone. "He was in the car over there," she says, pointing to a mound of concrete big enough to cover a school bus. "Can you see him?"

* * * * * * * * * * * * *

Some time after 2:00 a.m., Pierre-Richard and I are helping people near the hospital. There are doctors and nurses around, but they look like patients. Some are wounded, all look worried and lost. One whole wall of the building has collapsed, folded in on itself like a piece of disposable trash. It is not safe to go in the hospital, and the screaming is louder here, but not every cry is the same. Some are full of grief and sorrow, others are calling out to be rescued.

"Please help," says a man as he pulls us over to his wife. She is lying on the ground, her legs covered in blood. Her breathing is shallow, and I can tell that she doesn't have long to live. She's also heavily pregnant.

I want to tell the man that I can't help, but he pleads with me to do something, anything. I look him in the eye and know that he understands. He's not hoping for a miracle. He just can't face watching his wife die on his own.

She barely moves as I clean the blood from her legs, but the husband thanks me. And when I've done all I can, I don't feel that it's right to leave. I stay there and pray silently.

For the first time in hours the streets are finally quiet. I can't tell whether time is moving fast or slow, but when I next look at her, she's even weaker. It can't be long now.

Minutes pass.

Her breathing is shallow and rapid. Her husband buries his face in her hair.

I pray. *What do I do now, God?*

When I open my mouth to speak, I don't know exactly what I'm going to say. But I know the words will come. I take hold of the lady's hand, lean in close, and speak.

"I know you're hurting," I say. "I know you're in pain. But do you know that God is here in the midst of all this? He loves you so much that He took me and sent me here. He sent me here because He knows you and He loves you. It's not something to be taken lightly, but would you give your life to Him? Give Him your life."

I can see in her eyes that she has heard me, and I know deep down that she understands, and it takes all her effort to speak. But she tries.

"Yes," she says before she closes her eyes.

PART ONE

1

LONELY AND ALONE

Charlotte, N.C. Saturday, May 21, 2005. 10:49 p.m.

Is there a right time to start worrying when your husband doesn't come home at night? I guess it depends. On the night I sat alone in the house I shared with Michel, I decided on 11:00 p.m. That would be the point at which I would allow myself to panic.

I could easily have chosen an earlier time. Michel never stayed out late. Had he ever been out later than 10:00 p.m.? Or 9:00 p.m.? I couldn't remember. Sure, he'd spend most Saturday afternoons fixing cars and hanging with his friends. But that never lasted long. He didn't have the patience, and his friends didn't have the tools to do more than the most basic automobile repairs. I told myself that all my husband really needed each weekend was a few hours and a few beers to talk about whatever it is that men talk about on Saturday afternoons. And that was okay. Because Michel always came home. Always.

We'd been through some difficult times in the past, but it was my belief that we had finally settled into something good. So I had my own routines on a Saturday too. I'd clean for a while, then carry on grading the workbooks I'd brought home with me from school. Maybe I'd meet up with a girlfriend. If I did that, shoe shopping usually was involved at some point. And then I'd go home. Always.

Most Saturdays, if I walked in the door and he was there, I'd know. He didn't have to call out, and I didn't have to look for his shoes or coat by the stairs. All I needed to do was inhale and smell his cologne, now mixed with a little engine oil. Sounds strange, but I loved that smell. It warmed me like an open fire on a winter morning. I'd take off my shoes, go find him, and we'd embrace. After I'd show him the stack of papers I'd conquered or the new heels I'd purchased, we'd go out and eat.

Michel and Yvrose. Just another regular couple doing life in America.

But this particular Saturday in May was different. The pile of grading was bigger than usual, so there were no trips to the mall for me. I was sitting at the kitchen table when Michel left after lunch, and I stayed there all afternoon correcting fifth-grade French assignments. As the light faded from the sky, I pressed on, tackling the mountain of work in tiny steps.

It was a little before 8:00 p.m. when I looked up and allowed myself to realize that Michel had stayed out.

It was a little after 8:00 p.m. when I noticed the first waves of anxiety swirling within me.

I talked myself down. We hadn't argued. We hadn't fought. We didn't have money worries and we didn't have problems. Well, we didn't have any *new* problems. There were plenty of old ones, but life in the previous weeks had been settled. We'd been living in Charlotte for two years, and everything was good. We were even going to church. There was no reason at all for me to suspect that anything was wrong.

I decided to put a hold on worrying until it was late. Why worry about the impossible when any minute the door could open and I'd be hugging Michel hello again? So I carried on working, finished what I'd brought home from the previous night's meal at my favorite seafood restaurant, and felt my heart rate start to rise as the minute hand inched its way toward the top of the clock.

At 11:00 p.m. precisely, the fear unleashed itself. Without warning it exploded within me. I pushed away the books and the take-out box and called him on his cell. No reply. I hung up and immediately called him a second time. This time I hung around for the beep.

"Michel? Honey? It's me. I'm just wondering where you're at. You okay?"

The minutes dragged. I tried watching a little TV. That was no use. Flipping between *Desperate Housewives*, *America's Most Wanted*, and *Law and Order* killed my appetite. I tried going to bed but felt just as restless.

I dialed Michel again. I hung up when it reached voice mail.

It was midnight when I went back to my grading. I could only manage a few papers before my mind started to drift again. So I closed the books and paced a while up and down the kitchen. I checked the fridge. Tidied up a little. Glanced at my Bible.

And then I decided to dial the bank and check my balance.

The moment that I heard the automated teller inform me of my balance, all the breath in my lungs froze. My money—our money—gone. All of it.

Shaking, I punched buttons on my phone and retrieved more information. There had been a series of withdrawals earlier that evening at ATMs downtown. They had drained the account that Michel and I shared. Thousands of dollars that we had been saving ever since we turned our back on Florida and headed north. All gone.

I ended the call.

For a short while possible explanations lit up my mind like fireworks. Had someone stolen Michel's wallet and somehow got his code? Had he been forced at gunpoint to make the withdrawals himself? Or maybe he'd taken it out himself.

I dismissed them all and decided to stop trying to figure out what had happened. I knew that what mattered more was figuring out what I was going to do about it.

. . . .

This wasn't the first time I'd lost all my money. It wasn't even the first time that it had happened to me and Michel. In many ways the main reason we moved to Charlotte was because of what happened to us a few years earlier.

We were living in Boca Raton. Like so many people who had fled Haiti, we had found that South Florida was a natural place to settle. Our homeland felt closer down there, even though life in Florida was so different from Haiti that it might as well have been on a different planet. But whenever I stood and looked out at the ocean, it was almost possible to imagine that the lush green mountains and dusty roads of my homeland were just beyond the horizon. Or, at least, that we had not traveled so far that we had forgotten who we were or where we had come from.

Michel and I did what good immigrants do. We worked hard and made money. I was a nursing assistant at the time, and by living cheaply and squeezing every working hour out of the day, I was able to save a lot of money. I sent hundreds of dollars back home every month, and in the eight years since leaving Haiti, I had been able to save up tens of thousands of dollars.

I had a plan to turn it into hundreds of thousands of dollars. It was a good plan, too, and a friend joined me in the business. We rented a boat and filled it with all the items that we knew people were desperate to buy back in Haiti. Mattresses, beds, furniture, food, beer—we had it all on board, waiting to be delivered and sold at a handsome profit. And it would have all worked out as well, except the captain had a heart attack on the boat before reaching the Haitian coast. The captain died, and though the boat made it safely to port in Haiti, it was looted. In the space of a few hours, we lost everything.

That experience taught me a lot of different things. It taught me that it can take years to get you to the brink of success and moments to deliver you to the depths of disaster. It taught me that getting out of debt is a long and painful business and that there can be no substitute for hard work. It taught me that even though I was married, when everything came crashing down, I was pretty much on my own.

* * * * * * * * * * * *

When I woke up in Charlotte on Sunday morning and found that Michel still hadn't come home, I was ready to act. No more waiting around. No more being a victim. It was time to do something.

I phoned the police first, reporting Michel as missing. Then I called the bank again and got the details of all the ATMs where the money had been withdrawn. For a moment I was tempted to tell them I suspected we'd been robbed, but something stopped me. I wasn't ready to call it yet. In fact, the locations of the ATMs themselves told me everything I needed to know.

They were all within a few blocks of where he always spent his Saturday afternoons. I visited each one in turn, and even though I saw nothing unusual as I walked from one to the other—and saw no sign of Michel or any of his friends—somehow, I knew then that my husband had withdrawn the money himself. I don't know how I knew. But I knew.

Saturday evening had been dominated by a growing sense of panic about Michel; Sunday was given over to a growing sense of sorrow. A single question repeated within me. *Now what?* All this time, all these years, now what? After all that we'd saved, now what? After all our plans to open a business together, now what?

Piece by piece, I could feel the life that I had worked so hard to build begin to crumble.

Again…

. . . .

I was 17 when I first got pregnant. The father of the child was young like me, and the only response he had when I told him was to back away, shaking his head.

"You must get rid of it."

It. Not her or him. Not our child or the baby. Just *it.*

It was enough to reduce my world to dust. Whatever lay ahead of me, whatever choice I made, I knew then that I would face it alone.

I decided to keep the baby. I kept her secret as she grew within me. And when that became too difficult, I moved away from home, telling my parents I was moving to the mountains for a few months in order to work.

The mountains of Haiti are some of the most beautiful places on earth. Nothing comes close to the sight of the early morning sunshine picking out the tapestry of green that flows like a living ocean across the peaks. The weeks I spent there were some of the most wonderful I had ever known. As I felt this little life grow within me, everything around appeared more and more alive.

But the feelings did not last. I held her too few times before her life ended. And when that happened, my joy vanished.

I called her Moïka.

My father and mother had brought me up as a churchgoer. I had attended faithfully for many years. But in the pain that followed the loss of my baby, I never once considered turning to God for help. He was a stranger to me. Instead, I made a choice. I lost all interest in study, became a rebel, and looked for comfort in sex and drugs.

I didn't find much comfort. Though I learned to mask the pain, the ache of loneliness was never far from the surface. I tried my best to keep it away, but it was an impossible task. All it took was something like Michel disappearing for a night and a day to hurl me back into the pit.

. . . .

It was early on Sunday afternoon, and I was sitting at the kitchen table, staring blankly at the books. I heard the front door open and footsteps approach. Instinctively, I lifted my head and inhaled. I guess a part of me still hoped for Michel to walk in and give me a hug as if the previous 24 hours had never happened.

Michel stood in the kitchen doorway. Neither of us spoke. He looked tired. His clothes—the same ones he had gone out wearing the day before—looked tired. But it was the smell that shocked me. He did not smell of beer and cars and time spent laughing with friends. He smelled of burned rubber. I recognized it immediately.

When I had first moved to America, I lived with my brother Jean. He rented a room in an apartment in New York City and worked in a factory up in Connecticut that made windows and blinds. He was earning good money. Good money that he spent entirely on drugs. Jean would work all week and then burn through

$500,000 in a single night. If he worked enough overtime, he'd be able to keep on partying through Sunday as well. And by the time Monday morning came around, Jean would always be begging me for a few dollars for food.

Jean never sent any money home, and even if I gave him some cash on Monday, there was always a chance that he'd try to steal some from me by the end of Wednesday. He had no interest in anything but drugs, and when he wasn't high or I wasn't giving him money, we'd fight far worse than we ever did when we were kids growing up on the streets of Port-au-Prince.

"You should do society a service," I screamed one day. "Go throw yourself under a train."

For a moment I thought he was going to retaliate, but it passed. Jean grabbed his jacket and left, slamming the door and leaving the apartment with nothing more than the smell of burning rubber that clung to all his clothes.

Michel smelled exactly the same on this Sunday as I stared at him in the kitchen.

"You're on drugs," I said. "Crack?"

He didn't deny it.

I weighed my next words carefully, knowing they were dangerous.

"The police are going to return. They asked me to call them if you came back."

For the first time since he stepped inside the house, Michel stared at me. His eyes held both fear and anger. "You called them?"

In our culture if you call the police on someone, the relationship is over. No matter how long the friendship or how old the marriage. There are no questions, no explanations. It's just over.

I took a deep breath in. "Yes, I called them. I thought you were missing. I had no idea you were on drugs."

Michel spun on his heels, his body suddenly shot full of energy. I heard him run upstairs—two at a time—and begin hauling furniture around in the bedroom. By the time I reached him, he had pulled back the thick rug at the end of our bed and was lifting up a floorboard. I didn't say anything as he pulled out a pipe and a bag of drugs and pushed past me and into the bathroom. He emptied the bag and flushed it away, then covered his pipe in lighter fluid, lit it, and watched it burn in the sink.

When the flames had taken hold, he finally turned to me. There was no fear in his eyes anymore. Just anger.

"You know what this means?"

"I was worried," I said, my own temper starting to rise. "I was worried something had happened to you. That you'd done something stupid. Turns out I was right, wasn't I?"

He stared, trying to work out how much I knew.

I decided to save him the effort. "I know about the money."

He sat down on the edge of the bath. I hesitated for a moment, then went back downstairs.

* * * * * * * * * * * *

After almost a year of living with my crackhead brother, Jean, something remarkable had happened. He started seeing his ex-girlfriend from Haiti, Rachel. And not long after they hooked up again, one Saturday morning while Jean was sleeping in, she joined me in the kitchen and told me that she was going to ask him to marry her.

"Are you crazy? You know he's a drug addict?"

"I do," she said, pouring herself some coffee. "But God told me to do it."

I had to work hard not to laugh out loud. "God told you? Then your God needs to get His eyes tested, 'cause He ain't seeing things clearly."

Rachel tensed up, and I felt bad.

"I'm sorry. I didn't mean to offend you. But I don't want you to go through what I'm going through with him. It's like he's dead inside. I don't think anything can bring him back."

Rachel smiled, and the conversation ended.

Within months they were married, and I moved out. Jean phoned me a few weeks after the wedding.

He said he had quit taking drugs and that he had enrolled in theology school and wanted to apologize for everything he had put me through.

I couldn't find the words.

• • • • • • • • • • • •

Almost a decade had passed since Jean got married. He had long since stopped being known as Jean. He was Pastor Jean now, a living example of the power of God to change any life for the better. And the power of Rachel. A lot of people had seen his transformation and become Christians. Myself included. I started praying, found a church, and was trying to live my life rightly.

But it was hard.

As I sat in the kitchen while Michel remained in the bathroom, I prayed.

Michel wasn't the only one who needed help. I did too. So I told God that I was feeling desperate. I told Him that I was weak and didn't think I could face having to rebuild my life again. I told Him that if ever He was going to do a miracle for me, now was the time.

Michel came downstairs eventually. He sat at the table with me. He looked far older than a 40-year-old should.

"I really was worried about you," I said.

He looked at me. "I know." His face was impossible to read.

"I should call the police and tell them that you're safe."

He tensed but nodded.

I didn't really think about the words that came out of my mouth next, but I knew I wanted to forgive Michel for taking the money. I wanted him to change like my brother had.

"You know, my church has a treatment program that you can take. Or the police would probably let you go to rehab if you told them the truth."

The silence settled heavily like fog on the valley floor.

I waited as long as I could. "Michel? What do you want to do? Do you want to change?"

He shrugged.

"Call the police."

2

DREAMS AND VISIONS

Sometimes it can feel as though the path of life is set, that nothing can change it, that the years ahead of you will be just as full of sorrow and loneliness as the years before.

That was me.

I thought that pain was my lot in life, that suffering was my cross to bear. And down in the deepest part of me, I honestly believed I deserved it.

After the death of my beautiful baby girl, Moïka, I chose to numb the pain of losing her by losing myself in a world of alcohol and sex. I was 17—a child, really—but I quickly learned to do whatever it took to block out the darker feelings within me.

It was not long before I found out I was pregnant again. And when I did, no amount of partying on the streets of Port-au-Prince could block out the fear that gripped me inside. I was terrified that the same thing would happen again—that death was waiting.

Whenever I thought about the life growing inside me, the only future I could imagine was one in which I was weeping for the loss of another baby.

I could only see one way out. So I took it.

* * * * * * * * * * * *

Port-au-Prince, Haiti. 1980.

I was so nervous the day I visited the house of the doctor. From the outside, the house looked like any other in Haiti. Walls the color of mud. A worn iron roof patched with leaves and scraps of tarpaulin. A scraggy dog sniffing around outside with teats so old and swollen they almost scraped the ground as she walked.

The only difference was the window. Hardly any houses in Haiti had glass windows. Instead, they all had wooden shutters that would always be open during the day. But not the doctor's house. Her shutters were never open. Never.

The whole neighborhood knew why, of course, even though it was never discussed. The wooden shutters were closed to keep the noise of people's screams from leaking out onto the street. They didn't really work. Whenever I walked by and heard the muffled shout of pain coming from the doctor's house, like everyone else I would always lower my eyes and hurry my steps.

Everybody I knew pretended that what went on in the house didn't really happen. It was a secret that we all shared, but it was still a secret. Just like the fact that we all knew that the woman who lived in the house had never received any medical training. But we still called her the doctor all the same. I guess we found it reassuring.

On the morning of my appointment, I waited outside as long as I could, then pushed open the door and stepped into the darkness.

The doctor was waiting for me.

"Sit there," she said, pointing to a wooden bench low along the wall. There was another girl already sitting down. She looked about my age, maybe older. She didn't look at me as I sat beside her. She just stared at the space in front of her, an empty cup cradled in her hands which the doctor quickly snatched away.

I sat and watched while the doctor crouched in a corner and stirred a pan on a charcoal brazier.

"Drink this," she said, handing me the cup, which was now full of a hot tea the color of the earth outside. "And wait here."

She nodded at the girl next to me, who stood up and followed her through a curtain and into another room.

I knew the tea was full of herbs and pills and that it would start the process, but it took me a while to summon the courage to drink it. Eventually, I reminded myself of the truth of my situation. How I was once again living under my parents' roof, how they were still feeding me, and how telling them I was pregnant would wound them. I told myself I was not ready to be a mother, and that what I was about to do was the best thing for both of us. I forced myself to remember what it was like when Moïka died.

The same thing will happen again, I whispered as I lifted the cup to my lips. *This is my only choice.*

Soon after I drained it, the screams began in the next room.

Maybe other people would have left. But not me. I stayed, rooted to the rough wooden bench. I couldn't leave, even though the sounds were terrifying.

This is my only choice.

Eventually the girl came out. I couldn't look at her, but I felt her shadow leave the house. And I could feel the doctor's presence as well, even though she stayed on the other side of the curtain for a while. I closed my eyes and tried to think of something else, but no thoughts came. Instead, all I could focus on were the cramps gnawing deep within my belly.

Time dragged by. The cramps got worse. All I could do was concentrate on my breathing and try to ignore the pain.

I don't know how long I sat on the bench, gently rocking with my eyes shut tightly, but at some point, I was aware that I was not alone in the room anymore.

"Come," said the doctor.

I followed her through the curtain and into the room beyond. It was even darker in there, but beside the mat on the floor in the middle of the room, I could see the bloody rags and twisted coat hanger.

I did as I was told and lay down. I tried not to look at anything but the holes in the ceiling above me. I tried not to feel anything but the rough fibers of the mat beneath my palms. I tried not to smell anything except the mud floor and the stale sweat in the air. But it was no use. Once the doctor started her work, I could do nothing but scream.

* * * * * * * * * * * *

It is a cliché to say abortion kills more than the baby inside of you, but, in my case, it is also the truth. I returned to the doctor two more times over the next year, and with each visit to the same house with the same cup, the same bloody rags, I could feel the decay spreading further and further.

That's why, the fifth time I got pregnant, I stayed away. Not because I was choosing to keep the baby—I knew I had never been less able to be a mom. I chose to stay away from the doctor because I was terrified that if I went back I would die. I didn't know whether it was my body or my soul that I'd end up killing, but either way, I knew the risks were too high.

Even then, I still could not escape death. Before my pregnancy started to show, I miscarried.

I miscarried a second time a few months later.

And again.

And again.

Over the next 12 years I had 12 miscarriages. They followed me when I moved from Haiti to the U.S. They continued when I began my training to be a nurse and were the main reason why I abandoned nursing. They persisted even after I met, married, and tried to start a family with my husband, Michel. I had them when I was living the life of a rebel, and I had them when I was trying to live the life of a Christian. And every time they happened, I heard the same voice echoing within me…

You deserve this.

     •   •   •   •   •   •   •   •   •   •   •   •

Michel was a good husband at first. But the good times did not last. Early on in our marriage, I started to suspect that he was having an affair. I dismissed my fears at first. I did not want to believe that they could true.

But they were true.

One day when I was alone in the house, studying as usual, I heard his cell phone go off a number of times. He never left it behind, so I searched until I found it, wondering whether the messages might be from him trying to locate it.

They weren't.

They were from a woman. And they left me no room to doubt what was going on between them.

I confronted Michel when he returned home later that day. He admitted the affair and told me the lady was someone I knew. I threw him out that night.

Even before the door slammed and I heard his car speed off down the street, I heard the voice again.

You deserve this.

. . . .

A few days later I found out the name of the girl that Michel was having an affair with. She was a girl 20 years younger than him and barely able to drink legally. I knew her from church, and the pain I felt when he told me was like another twist of rusted, jagged metal within me.

I'd been going to church ever since my brother had been saved from his drug addiction, and I carried on attending. But I didn't find any peace and healing there. I only found more pain. Michel and his girlfriend showed up most weeks too. I'd try to keep my distance and not look at her, but I could feel her eyes on me. When the service would end and the congregation would stand around talking about the week over cups of weak coffee, she'd be there, hanging onto his arm and smiling at me.

Most of the time she kept away from me, but one time she came right up and stood in front of me. Her smile was still perfect, and her head was cocked to one side as she looked me up and down, the way a zookeeper looks at a new addition.

"You're a mule," she said.

I didn't understand.

"You," she said, still smiling. "You can't give him children. You're only good for one thing—work. You know, like a mule."

She turned and left. I could feel all the light and life drain from my body.

And there was the voice again.

You deserve this.

. . . .

There was worse to come. Two months after Michel left, he was back at my door. He looked pale, ill, and old.

"I just heard from my ex-wife," he said as he stood looking weak and tired on the doorstep. "She has AIDS. She's dying."

I'd not been sleeping well before that, and I'd lost almost 50 pounds in a few weeks. But this latest news rocked me in ways I'd never experienced before. My life took another twisted descent into the darkness. I started having diarrhea. Within days I got myself tested. The initial result was negative, but even that wasn't much relief. I had to wait another six months before I could have a follow-up test and receive my official results.

All along the voice was there. In the darkness at night when I could not sleep, and in the daytime when I could not get my brain to focus on the work that I needed to do—it was there. Cold. Accusing. Familiar.

You deserve this.

⠂ ⠂ ⠂ ⠂ ⠂ ⠂ ⠂ ⠂ ⠂ ⠂ ⠂ ⠂

One week after I discovered that Michel had spent all our savings on crack, I said goodbye to him. I watched him pull his backpack out of the trunk of the car, sling it over one shoulder, and walk into the rehab center in which the police had helped him enroll.

I had no idea what to expect. I knew what I hoped and prayed for—that beyond the doors of the facility my husband would find the same degree of miraculous healing and transformation that my brother Jean had found. But if life had taught me anything, it was that true change is rare.

I didn't know what to do with myself, so I pulled out my cellphone and dialed a number Jean had given me the day before. He had asked me to call it and speak to a woman who was in town for the weekend and wanted to go to church. Her name was Mary, or Marianne, or something.

"Hello?"

"Oh, hey," I said. "My brother, Pastor Jean, gave me your number. Said you were in Charlotte this weekend and wanted to go visit a church?"

"Yes," said the voice on the end of the line. "I'd like that."

She sounded nice, and I wasn't in the mood for shoe shopping or schoolwork. "Would you like to meet today? I don't have much planned, just a few errands."

"I'd like that too," she said.

She told me where she was staying with her friend, and we made a time to meet and said goodbye.

That was it. Less than two minutes long and barely more than a hundred words. But I'll never forget it. It was the phone call that changed my life.

• • • • • • • • • • • •

Her name was not Mary or Marianne, but Marie. And from the moment she first opened the door and I saw her—looking like a wild-eyed street magician but with a presence soaked in God's peace and radiance—I knew she was unlike any person I had ever met. Right from the moment we met, a unique bond formed.

Marie had been born in Haiti, just like me. We'd both spent almost 20 years living in the U.S. as well, never straying far from the East Coast. But the similarities stopped there. I was bruised and scarred from life, weighed down by guilt, and waiting for another thing to go wrong. Marie was the polar opposite. Marie was free.

It was almost summer, and the moment Marie and I walked to my car it felt as if winter vanished. The light seemed brighter, warmer, and clearer. And for a moment, as we sat in my kitchen drinking coffee and she told me all about her reason for being in Charlotte—how she was accompanying a friend from

Massachusetts who was in town to visit the seminary—I wondered if she was, in fact, an angel.

It was a question I'd ask myself many times over the coming weeks.

"Do you want to know the strange thing, Yvrose? Even though I'm only here for two nights, when I was packing I kept on adding more and more things to my suitcase. I said to God, 'Hey, this is strange, isn't it? I'm visiting for the weekend, but I'm taking enough clothes for a month. Are You going to tell me what's going on here?' He didn't." Marie took a sip of coffee and let a smile spread across her face. "But that's okay. I like it when I can't figure out what He's up to. You hear me?"

Not being able to figure out what God was up to was not at the top of my list of favorite things. In fact, it was one of the worst things in my life. I hated feeling as though God was playing with me, the way a kid pulls the wings off flies. Yet I managed a half smile and nodded.

"Oh, I hear you."

There was a silence between us, but it wasn't awkward or strange. I didn't feel that I needed to fill it. I was happy just to be near Marie. She was cradling her coffee cup in both hands, a smile spread wide across her face as she looked out the kitchen window onto the yard out back.

How could it be that this person I had only met a few hours earlier suddenly felt so important to me? The connection was unlike any I'd ever experienced.

Eventually, Marie put the cup down and turned to me. "Do you know what I believe?" When she spoke, her voice was different. Softer, quieter. When she first came in, she'd been loud and full of life and vitality and mischief. Now her words sounded like a distant echo of thunder, miles and miles away. Firm. Immovable. Mighty. "I believe that God is in control here. Do you?"

I half nodded. Since Jean became a Christian, I had never had a problem believing that God was in control. How else could my brother's life have been turned around so dramatically? What I struggled with was believing that God being in control was a *good* thing for my life. After all this pain and struggle, I'd come to view God as a distant, stern, maybe even cruel power in my life.

But here was a woman who did not run for cover when God spoke. Instead she packed her bags and went exactly where He told her to go. I was fascinated and stunned. With a few words, Marie awakened an appetite deep within me that I'd never experienced before. I wanted to see God differently. I wanted to believe like she did. I wanted to know that God being in control was not something I had to fear.

"Marie," I said, but no more words came. I knew what I wanted but didn't know how to ask for it. As we sat in silence, I felt something I had not sensed for far too long. I felt peaceful.

I looked up. Marie's eyes were closed, her face turned toward the window. There was a glow about her I'd not noticed before. She was praying. Part of me wanted to stare, but the hunger for whatever she had was too great.

I closed my eyes and joined her in prayer.

* * * * * * * * * * * *

And so began the strangest and most wonderful month in my life.

We spent hours praying that day.

And we spent hours praying the next day as well. Marie was supposed to be returning to Massachusetts with her friend, but when she announced that she had decided not to go back right away, I was not at all surprised. I told her that she was welcome to stay with me for as long as she wanted. She said she'd like that, and then we went back to praying.

I learned more about how to pray in that first weekend than I had in all the years I'd been going to church. Marie taught me about how to wait on God, how to be guided by Him, and how to fight the battles I could not fight physically. She taught me how to confess and how to accept God's grace and forgiveness. Most of all, she taught me what it meant to be in the place where there were as few barriers as possible between God and me.

I'd come home from my day at school and find her in the kitchen. She'd have started preparing dinner, and we'd talk as we worked together. Soon we'd be praying. Often, by the time the food was ready, we'd be too deep in prayer and too full of the presence of God to want to break.

Before I knew it, a month had passed, and Marie was telling me that she really did need to return home. I felt a temptation to panic at the thought of being alone again, especially as Michel was due back from rehab in a few days. How would things be between us? How could I begin to explain the riches of this new life I'd discovered? Worse, what if everything returned to normal, to the way it used to be between us?

Marie helped me to pray about it and taught me how to resist the temptation to panic. And by the time she left, I felt peaceful. As I closed the door after waving goodbye, I walked through the empty rooms. The house didn't feel so different after all—Marie had gone, but God had not.

               ● ● ● ● ● ● ● ● ● ● ● ● ●

A day after Marie left, I was in my bedroom, praying. I started feeling restless and had the urge to search around in the pile of stuff that Michel kept beneath his side of the bed. It was mainly just odd socks, old newspapers, and a couple of storage boxes with old photos inside. But at the very bottom of the pile I found something that made my mouth go dry and my heart start to race.

It was a hardback book. There was no dust jacket and the markings on the cover were faded, but I recognized them immediately. I picked up the book the way you pick up a dead snake—cautiously, slowly, alert to danger.

Almost everyone in Michel's family had been involved in witchcraft in some way. Michel was no exception. When we first met he was a Mason and, like so many other people in Haiti, he saw nothing wrong in visiting a voodoo priest if he was in trouble. But I always had the feeling that Michel's heart was not deeply given over to such darkness. So, when Michel started coming with me to church and swore that he had turned his back on it, I believed him.

The book in front of me proved I'd been wrong. It was a Masonic book, and it only took me a few seconds to discover it was full of prayers, enchantments, and the kind of darkness I wanted to keep far, far away.

I took it out back and burned it.

* * * * * * * * * * * *

I didn't confront Michel about the book when he returned home. Perhaps if he had stayed around longer, we might have discussed it. As it was, Michel soon returned to his old ways. It almost felt inevitable when he stayed out late one night, leaving me at the kitchen table, waiting.

The smell was obvious the moment he came through the door.

"You're not clean, are you?"

He shrugged.

"Were you clean at rehab?"

Michel stared at me. "No."

I sighed. I wasn't surprised. In fact, I was almost grateful. At least this way it was clear what needed to happen.

"Either you go back to rehab and do it properly, or you leave."

Michel nodded. "I'd rather leave."

The next morning, he packed three bags and left. I have not seen him since.

・　・　・　・　・　・　・　・　・　・　・　・

It took almost a week of living alone in the house before I realized something incredible had happened. At any other time in my life, seeing Michel walk out would have led me down into the darkness. I would have felt shame clawing at my heart, and the old voice telling me I deserved this would have returned—loud, cold, and impossible to silence.

Not this time.

I was sad that Michel had gone, sad that he was still held hostage by his addictions. But that sadness was quiet and small within me. There was no shame attached to it, no guilt. Instead, my head and my heart were full.

Ever since Marie had left, I'd been having dreams. These were not the usual kind where my mind was trying to fix the problems that troubled me during the day. These were different. They were clearer than any dream I'd had before. I could see faces as if I were awake and they were in front of me. I could see the land as if I were standing in the middle of it. The only thing I wasn't totally clear about was what the dreams meant.

The dreams occurred over a number of nights, and I knew they were all connected. In one of them, I was standing on top of a mountain. I was fishing, somehow able to reach all the way down to the waters that lay at the base of the slopes. I'd catch a fish and then haul it up to me. But every time I got it close, the fish fell from the hook and tumbled all the way back down to the water. It bugged me, especially because I was hungry and wanted to eat.

In another dream, I was back on the mountaintop, still fishing but this time without a line. As I watched, a great shoal of fish rose up out of the water, surged through the air toward me, and landed right by my feet. Instead of being amazed that the fish were flying through the air toward me, I was just deeply happy and content.

One night, I dreamed that I was walking along a rocky patch of land. I knew I had a clear, specific purpose—that I was looking for something. It was only when I saw a shack made out of wood and dried palm leaves that I found what I was searching for. I walked up to an old woman sitting in the dust in front of the hut and spoke to her. "I need to find a place I can use as a school. Can I use your home?"

She said no, and I carried on searching.

More people said no, but still I searched, crossing the rocky ground and asking everyone I saw if they could help. Finally, I found a woman who did not reject me. She was standing outside the most broken down, filthy house I'd seen. But she said yes, and right away I began cleaning the place.

Why was I preparing a school? Only when I asked myself that question did I look up and see them—a crowd of children, all running around while I worked. I'd not noticed them before, but as soon as I saw them I knew they were the reason I was there. And I knew that they needed me.

I stopped working and looked at them more closely. They were all half naked, barefoot, and covered in filth. I'd never seen such poverty. I'd never seen children like them.

Who would want to be around these kids?

The question echoed loudly inside me. But the answer was louder:

I do. I want to be with them.

3

TWO MIRACLES IN HAITI

A few months had passed since Michel left, and I had been able to save a little money. Not much compared to the thousands he had taken, but a few hundred dollars was better than a few cents. I was glad I had saved when, shortly after Thanksgiving, I found out that my mother had been diagnosed with a heart condition and was dying in a hospital in Haiti. I dropped everything and bought a ticket on the first flight out of Charlotte.

Even though I never completed my full nursing training, I have spent enough time in hospitals and around doctors and nurses to feel comfortable among them. The smell of disinfectant, the buzz of the strip lighting, the way the background noise hums with energy like a hive of worker bees—these all comfort me. Whenever I'm in a hospital, I notice myself exhale a little.

Almost every first-time visitor who leaves the U.S. and steps out of the airport at Port-au-Prince has a memory of being shocked by a stark difference between Haiti and home. Even though they are still in the same time zone as the eastern seaboard, many feel as though a whole world has fallen away. They stare, struggling to believe that somewhere so close to home can be so different. For some it is the amount of trash on the streets. Others can't get over the depth of the darkness that covers the land once night falls. Some stare at the state of the roads and the cars, others at the state of the people. But for me, the clearest memory of feeling shocked by the poverty of my homeland is the memory of walking into the hospital where my mother lay dying.

At first, I hoped it would not be too bad. Mom was in a private hospital, and the few dollars it cost each day was a small price to pay for not having to go to the general hospital. As I waited to be allowed in, I realized I'd forgotten that in Haiti receiving medical care in a hospital is a privilege—a solemn occasion which is handled with respect. I lined up alongside people who were hoping to have their long-awaited tests and appointments, wearing their best clothes and most serious expressions. Dressed in their faded blouses and patched leather shoes, they shuffled toward the gates and the guards who patrolled them like it was a military facility.

Inside the hospital felt like war.

The temperature was over 100 degrees, and the air was thick with the smell of infection. I walked by patients lying on the floor and slumped against walls, many with open wounds unattended. Between the swarms of flies and the smell of bacteria feasting on flesh, it was almost possible to pick out the worst cases.

I wanted to stop and help, to find a nurse and offer my services. But I also wanted to run and find my mom, checking that she was still alive.

I found her in a private room. As I looked at Mom sleeping peacefully, I exhaled. The bare concrete floor was dirty and there was no medical equipment to speak of, but at least she was alive. And even though I knew that her risk of infection was high, I was grateful to be able to close the door behind me and keep the worst of the hospital's cases away.

Mom's condition was serious, and she'd been given a week or two to live. After a lifetime of surviving in the chaos of Port-au-Prince, and years of her underlying condition remaining untreated, her heart was giving out. Breathing was a struggle.

As I hugged her, she felt bird-boned, and I knew there wasn't long to go.

＊ ＊ ＊ ＊ ＊ ＊ ＊ ＊ ＊ ＊ ＊ ＊

My brothers and I had arranged for one of us to always be with her, and over the coming days Jean, Telfort, and I each spent hours sitting beside her bed. From time to time she would whisper a few words and squeeze my hand, but mostly she slept and I prayed.

One night, when it was late enough for the heat to have eased a little, I noticed something new in the air. It was a smell that I'd never encountered—as if all the infections in the hospital had been thrown on a fire that was filling the air with acrid smoke. "That smells like death," I murmured, and for a moment I wondered whether they were burning bodies somewhere.

Deep within me I knew there was more to it than that.

Death is here.

The phrase flooded my mind. I had the strongest sense that God was telling me these words.

Before I could think or pray more about it, Mom was squeezing my hand and trying to speak.

I leaned over and put my ear to her mouth.

"I need the bathroom," she said.

It took time to help her out of bed and down the corridor to the room with the long drop toilet. By the time I got her back on the bed, the effort had exhausted her. A look of fear fell across her eyes, and she moved her mouth to speak but no words came. Her mouth was so dry and cracked, but drinking didn't seem to help at all. She could barely sip, let alone swallow.

"It's okay, Mama," I said, easing her back onto the bed. "It's okay. I love you."

She closed her eyes and slipped out of consciousness for a while. Her breathing sped up—rapid, shallow breaths as if she was snatching at life. I'd seen enough people die to know that she would not last long.

Her eyes rolled back, and I held my breath.

Death is here.

The thought returned, only this time it wasn't like before, not like a revelation or an insight. This time it felt like a battle call. The enemy was at the gates. It was time to fight.

I let go of Mama's hand and lay down on the floor.

"God," I prayed out loud, ignoring the feel of the dirt against my skin and the smell of filth. "You just revealed to me the smell of death. You told me that Mama's time is almost over. Why would You show me that if You were not going to do something about it?"

I could feel the words rise within me, like a mountain wind that suddenly picks up. I didn't know where I was heading, but I knew I needed to pray and not stop.

"When You stopped by Abraham, You told him You were going to destroy the cities, but because Abraham was Your friend, You spared his nephew. So I am going to pray for my mama. I know that she is sick. I know that she will die sometime. But I pray in the name of Jesus, let nobody die in this hospital tonight."

The moment those last words were out, I knew that they were not my own. I had enough faith to believe that God could save my mom, but to go a whole night without anyone at all dying in the hospital? Only God could have planted an idea so wild.

I lay on the floor for the longest time.

Let nobody die in this hospital tonight.

The words came back to me like waves on a shore. They were not mine, but I believed them all the same. I was like an instrument in an orchestra, adding a small sound to a much larger symphony, at all times led by the conductor in front.

Nothing distracted me. Not the smell of cold concrete nor the days-old dirt spread out beneath me. I prayed, lying flat on the floor for what felt like an hour but could easily have been more.

And then, just as quickly as it had all begun, the moment shifted. I became aware of the gentle noises of hospital life beyond the door. I sat up, looked over at Mama, and saw her breathing calmly, sleeping peacefully.

My prayers became my own again, and I cried as I thanked God for keeping death away from her. I was restless, though. I knew that my prayers on the floor hadn't been only for my mom but for everyone in the hospital, so after I checked on my mom carefully, I slipped through the door into the corridor.

My eyes were drawn to a young woman on a mat up against the wall. She was feverish, curled up like a baby, rocking herself back and forth. The air was thick with the smell of whatever infection raged inside her.

I stood at her side and prayed. I did not reach for my own prayers or try to find my own words. I simply tried to join in with the chorus of prayer that I had sensed back in Mama's room. To whatever God was doing, I simply said, "Amen."

The young woman calmed a little, and in time I sensed it was right to move on. I walked throughout the hospital, asking God to show me who to pray for. There were old and young, people who looked as though death was waiting to snatch them, and some whose eyes were rigid with fear. With each of them, I prayed the same prayer—a prayer I had heard Marie say so many times before. "On earth as it is in heaven."

I did not sleep at all that night, but I was not tired at all when the doctor came to check on my mom the next morning. She was sitting up in a chair, breathing comfortably, and the doctor said he could not believe she was the same woman he had seen the day before.

"If you feel like this tomorrow," he said, shaking his head, "you might as well go home."

He started to leave but paused at the door. When he didn't speak, I jumped in.

"Doctor, did anyone else improve last night?"

He looked at me, confused at first. Then his face softened. "Yes. Lots of them."

"And did anybody die?"

He bit his lip and shrugged. "Nobody."

. . . .

In the months between Marie returning to Massachusetts and me returning to Haiti, my dreams had continued. If anything, they became more vivid. They reappeared at night, sometimes a repeat of a previous dream, but sometimes new parts of the scene were revealed. And they often flicked in and out of my mind during the day. Even when I wasn't asleep I was able to see the images of poor, ragged children, dusty ground, and broken-down buildings. It was as if my brain couldn't get enough time processing them when I was asleep. It needed to examine them in the light as well.

As I walked out of the hospital that morning, my mind was flooded with one image in particular: a map.

I had first seen it a few months earlier. I woke up in the morning with a clear impression of a mountain that ran straight down to the ocean. I could see the contours of the land, the curve of the coastline, and the way that the palm trees were scattered like soldiers. It was so vivid and clear that as soon as I could, I drew it out by hand.

Intuitively and instantly, I knew two things about the map.

I knew it was a real place. And I knew that wherever it was, the location played a part in God's plan for my life.

I kept the map in my purse and would take it out from time to time. I tried looking at other maps to see if I could work out the location, and because it felt like the map dream was linked to the dreams about the children and the school, I focused my searching on Africa. But nowhere seemed to fit. No matter where I looked, whether online or in printed atlases, I couldn't find anywhere in Africa where two countries were separated by an ocean in the way I had seen in my dream.

The moment I said goodbye to my mom and walked out of the hospital, I knew that I had been searching in the wrong place. I needed to look in Haiti.

*　　*　　*　　*　　*　　*　　*　　*　　*　　*　　*　　*

My younger brother, Telfort, has a smile that could power a whole village. Even when he's not particularly happy, his mouth will break into a grin at a moment's notice. He was a mean soccer player when he was younger, and whenever he scored a goal, his celebrations were so full of joy that the opposing team couldn't help smiling too.

But when I told Telfort about my dreams and showed him my map as we stood outside the hospital, he frowned.

I couldn't figure out his reaction. Like me, Telfort had left Haiti when he was younger, but he'd not made a home for himself in the U.S. He always said he preferred Haiti, despite life being so much harder here. After a few years of feeling restless as an immigrant in

America, he returned and made a life for himself here, setting up businesses and trading all over the country. There wasn't a part of Haiti he hadn't visited. And if he didn't recognize my map as belonging to our homeland, then I was sure that my hunch was wrong.

He stared at the map—tattered and creased from overuse—as if it was a crucial piece of evidence in a crime.

"Telfort?"

Still nothing. He chewed his lip and deepened his frown.

"You're sure this is the ocean?"

"Yes," I said.

A little more silence and staring.

"No," he said eventually. "There's nowhere in Haiti exactly like it." He looked at me, reading my disappointment. "But I think you might be wrong about the ocean."

Two hours later, Telfort and I were heading east, driving along the road that led straight to the border with the Dominican Republic. After an hour of sitting in traffic, we finally crawled free from the city, and Telfort's sedan picked up as much speed as it could as he threaded his way through the usual spread of potholes and broken-down vehicles.

Telfort had explained his theory about the ocean not being an ocean. I was having a hard time believing it, but he seemed convinced.

"You're sure you don't remember going to Lake Azuei?"

"No," I repeated. "And anyway, in all the dreams I've had, the water stretches out to the horizon. It's way too big to be a lake."

A grin started to form on my brother's mouth.

"What?"

"Nothing, sis."

"Tell me."

Telfort slowed down to avoid an ambling cow. "The lake's pretty big, believe me."

I wanted to believe him. I wanted to know that my instincts were right about where God was leading me. And after what happened in the hospital the night before, I was feeling able to trust that God was speaking.

But Haiti? I'd spent months thinking I was being called to Africa—perhaps to help support a school out there, or even set one up myself. Yet if Telfort was right and my map resembled this corner of Haiti, then where would I be? How would I work out where it was that God wanted me to be? How would I know for sure?

. . . .

"See what I mean?"

From the corner of my eye, I knew Telfort was looking at me, but my vision was locked straight ahead. The road had taken a couple of wide sweeps, first to the left and then the right. Instantly, the view through Telfort's cracked windshield changed. Instead of the usual rocks and roads that we'd been looking at for the previous hour, we were now driving alongside a lake so large that if you looked in a certain direction it was impossible to see the other side.

I could feel my heart quicken, the way it always used to speed up before a test at school. The lake was big enough, and there was something about it that felt familiar. But there were still no mountains around us, and my dreams had been very clear about them.

We slowed down as the road took us through the town of Fond Parisien. It was a typical sight for Haiti. Single-story houses stuck to the side of the road. Older men in vests and gum boots sat in the dust and stared. Women carried impossible loads on their heads. Young men stood beside tables made of thin branches selling gasoline in plastic bottles. None of it had been in my dream, but still my heart beat loud and fast within me.

Telfort was looking at me more than he was looking at the road now. I could feel his smile as we entered another bend in the road, but I was still not convinced. The lake was big, but the mountains were unmis–

"That is not possible!" The words flew from my mouth like a tornado. "Telfort! Look!"

Ahead of us was a mountain so tall I had to lean forward in my seat if I wanted to see the top. At the bottom it tumbled straight into the lake. Exactly as I'd seen in my dream.

Exactly.

4

THE MOUNTAIN AND THE OCEAN

And there's the tree. See it?"

Telfort shook his head. "Amazing. You're sure you've never been here before?"

I smiled. "Not in person."

From the moment we'd turned the corner and seen the mountain, I'd been able to direct Telfort. It was like going back to a childhood home, the kind of experience you get when the memories are a little dusty and hazy with the passing years but then flood back with every familiar sight.

Soon we were parking beneath the lone pine tree that stood in the middle of the village.

"You want me to kill the engine?"

"Sure," I said, getting out and taking a good look around me.

It was exactly as I'd seen it in all my dreams. There were maybe 200 homes, all made in the traditional style with mud walls and dried palm leaves for a roof. None were much bigger than Telfort's car.

Even by Haitian standards, the village was poor. The earth was rockier than usual, and though the lake looked big enough to keep an army of fishermen in business, a handful of aging wooden fishing boats lay dry by the water's edge.

Telfort joined me in looking across the lake. He pointed out the couple of parts where the coastline was in the territory of the Dominican Republic. "It's been overfished. We blame the Dominican Republic and they blame us. Who knows which one of us is really to blame. But what we do know is that most boats you see out there will be smuggling rather than fishing."

When strangers drive into a remote village in Haiti, the reaction is normally the same. The adults will hang back and stare, and the kids will run up to see if they can hustle a little food or water. Not this village. It was about as lifeless as the lake. We had passed a few people when we'd driven in, but not nearly as many as I expected.

"Look," said Telfort, pointing to a home nearby. It was typical, with a small front yard the size of a king-size bed out front. Through the gaps in the border fence, woven out of twigs and thin branches, I could see what Telfort was pointing to—a child staring at us.

I walked over, hoping that I didn't scare the child. The child was naked from the waist up, and I guessed around five or six years old. A boy? Maybe. I couldn't tell.

"Hey," I said once close enough. Even though my mom still spoke Creole, the words sounded strange coming from my mouth. "What's your name?"

The child said nothing.

"I'm Yvrose."

Still nothing.

"You want some water?"

The child stared, then slowly edged out from behind the fence. As soon as I saw him it was my turn to be dumbstruck.

I knew the child. I recognized him the way I recognized my own brothers. He was one of the children I'd seen in my dreams. He was wearing the same ragged pants, had the same distended belly and copper-toned hair that spoke of malnutrition. And just like in my dreams, he remained silent, his eyes locked on mine.

I gave him my bottle of water and forced some deep breaths to steady myself.

"Okay, God," I prayed under my breath. "You've got my attention. What do You want me to do?"

. . . .

"Yvrose!"

I turned around to see Telfort standing at the car, an old woman next to him. I smiled at the boy, who returned the smile with his own watery, cheesy grin, and then I walked back to the car.

"Mama," I said, using the typical greeting for an older woman in Haiti. "What is the name of this village?"

"Fonds Baillard."

"We're looking for a church. Is there one here?"

She looked at me carefully, a little confused. Had my accent really changed that much after living in the U.S.? I repeated my question, a little slower this time.

She paused, still sizing me up. Eventually, she decided in my favor. "Follow me," she said, leading Telfort and me down a narrow path that twisted around the backs of several houses.

The moment she stopped and pointed at a typical house with a red rag tied to the roof, Telfort and I stopped, inhaled, and looked at each other. There was no trace of a smile on my brother's face. We both knew that this was no church. In Haiti, the red flag outside a house only ever means one thing—it is the home of a voodoo priest.

Before we could do anything, the old woman had called out and asked whomever lived there to come and meet us.

The man who shuffled out was easily as old as the woman. His eyes were yellow and his skin as creased and worn as old leather boots. But as he looked Telfort and me up and down, he didn't seem threatening or someone from whom we needed to flee. He just looked kind.

"Is there a school in this village?"

He shook his head and frowned. "These people have nothing," he said. He seemed genuinely saddened by the fact.

"Nothing?"

Again he shook his head. This time he stiffened a little. "These people have nothing to offer you."

"Oh no," I said, "I don't want anything from them. Nothing at all."

The old voodoo priest tilted his head and looked at me for the longest time. The more he stared, the more peaceful I felt. God had guided my steps so far that day, getting me all the way to the village that I'd been dreaming about for months. It wasn't hard to believe that this conversation with this voodoo priest was one God wanted me to have.

The smile returned to his face. "I'm the one who gives them something to eat from time to time. Whatever you need, I can help you."

Without really thinking about it, I reached out and grabbed his hand. It was cold, and I could easily feel the bones. "I'm Yvrose. I'm a Christian, and I know that God sent me here for these people. They are not forgotten. God remembers them. Good things are coming to them."

I could feel his hand start to tremble a little. He let out a little sigh, and his eyes became those of a hungry child.

"If there's anything that's being given out, don't forget me."

I couldn't help laughing. "Oh, I won't. You know, when it rains, it rains on everybody. God loves you as much as He loves these other people. I promise you that every good thing that is going to happen to this place will be made open to you too. And believe me, you're going to want to give your life to Jesus before long."

He stared at me a while. I wondered if I'd said too much. But truth is truth, and I wanted him to know my exact reason for being there.

"Come," he said, a smile returning to his face. "I want to show you something."

·   ·   ·   ·   ·   ·   ·   ·   ·   ·   ·   ·   ·

The tears started flowing as soon as I saw it. It wasn't strong enough to be called a building, and it seemed that even the lightest gust of wind or shallowest of floods would tear it down. With its blue tarp sheets stretched tightly over a frame of twisted, rotten sticks, it looked more like a makeshift den than a place where young lives would be prepared for the future. But there it was, the only school in the village.

It wasn't the fragility of the building that made me cry. It was its familiarity.

Just like the mountain and the lake, the pine tree and the little boy, I'd seen this place in my dreams. The only difference was that as I stood beside the voodoo priest, my brother, and the old lady and looked at the school, I knew I was looking at the answer to the question echoing within me for months.

I'd wanted to know why. Why was God giving me these dreams?

Why was He showing me these people and this place and stirring me up like this? And—for the past hour, ever since Telfort and I had turned the corner outside Fond Parisien—why was God leading me to this place, on this day?

And here was my answer.

I was here to help the school.

I hadn't heard an audible voice or seen bright lights shining down. But I knew that this was what God wanted. I knew it the way you know that when you take your next breath in, your lungs will fill with the oxygen you need to survive. I knew it the way you know gravity will hold the cup that you place on a table. This knowledge went so deep that it instantly and completely answered my question.

So even before I took one step toward the school or spoke to the woman who was crouched in the dirt, boiling water on a charcoal fire, I knew that I was all in. I knew I was prepared to do anything I could to help.

"Teacher. This lady has come to help," the voodoo priest said. With that, he and the old woman turned away and left Telfort and me alone with her.

My own classroom in Charlotte could not have been more different. Back in the U.S., I had desks and chairs, computers, and a video screen. I could use anything I wanted to teach my French classes—film, music, textbooks—and when the bell rang and I went home for the day, someone would clean my room.

In front of me was nothing much more than a mud floor and fragile walls. There were just two wooden benches, both broken and unable to stand properly, and an old chalkboard that was too wrecked and broken to write on more than one-third of it. I could not see any books or pens, no posters or resources of any kind.

Although I guessed she was in her early thirties, the teacher looked more tired and worn out than anything else. She stood up and shook my hand, but even her grip was fading.

For a moment, I considered telling her about everything that had been going on with me—about the dreams and my mother getting healed the day before and the map and the drive from Port-au-Prince that morning, but I knew it was too much. You don't give a person who hasn't eaten for a month a three-course meal.

I decided to take it slowly. "Can we sit and talk for a moment?"

She nodded, and Telfort and I sat on one of the benches while she took the other. Every time one of us shifted, the bench wobbled as if ready to collapse. If the teacher noticed, she didn't seem to mind.

After we had introduced ourselves and found out her name was Cecile, I asked her to tell me about the school.

She puffed air into her cheeks and looked away. I wondered if even that was too much to ask, but she relaxed and looked back at me.

"This is where the church meets. Last year they saw that the village needed a school. Because I grew up here and nearly finished high school, they asked me to become the teacher."

I knew this was nothing unusual, and most schools in Haiti would have teachers without degrees or any real qualifications. But it still shocked me that this one village was relying on someone who hadn't even finished high school. "Nearly finished?"

"My parents could not afford for me to carry on."

"How old are you, Cecile?"

"Twenty-three."

I tried to hide my surprise, but I know she registered it. She smiled weakly.

"I have been teaching here for the last four months. It has not been easy. When I started, there were 26 children, but the parents don't pay the school fees, so the children have to stop coming."

"How many do you have now?"

"Six."

This was typical. Without any government support, schools in Haiti have to charge pupils to attend, otherwise they would not be able to pay their teachers. So if parents don't pay, the children are not allowed to attend. It sounds brutal, but if schools allow pupils to skip payments, then pretty soon the schools die.

That wasn't what bothered me. With only six pupils paying, there would not have been enough money to cover Cecile's salary.

"Are you getting paid?"

For the first time, Cecile looked me straight in the eye. "No," she said. "I have not been paid."

"Since when?"

"I have not been paid. Not since I started four months ago. But I want to teach these children and I want to help. That's why I stay."

I wanted to hug her and burst into tears at the same time. We were both teachers, but I got frustrated when my classroom didn't get cleaned. Would I still turn up for work if I missed four paychecks in a row?

I didn't have to think hard about what I did next. I didn't have to talk it through or give time for the plan to develop. I didn't have to go away and pray about it. I knew that God had brought me there to meet with Cecile and that He had laid out in front of me the clearest invitation I had ever been given—to help.

From my bag I pulled enough money to cover Cecile's missing wages—which was less than the price of a pair of heels.

"I want you to have this," I said. "But I also want you to know that I'm coming back. God has been leading me on a journey, and I know that this is where I'm supposed to be helping. So, if you'll have me, I'd like to do what I can to support you. Is that okay?"

Cecile nodded. We hugged. Telfort's laughter filled the whole village.

. . . .

That afternoon I went shopping with Telfort in Port-au-Prince. We filled the trunk of his car with school supplies, everything from a new chalkboard and books to rulers, pencils, crayons, and paper. He had promised to take them back to Cecile the next day and to keep on visiting every month to deliver her wages while I was back in Charlotte, trying to figure out what the next step of the journey would look like for me.

In truth, I already knew. That's why I couldn't wait until I was back in the U.S. to phone Marie.

I called her from Haiti the next morning as I waited to board my plane.

"Marie? I found the place that has been in all those dreams. It's here in Haiti, just by the border."

"Oh yes!" Her scream of delight was so loud I almost dropped the phone. "We're coming!"

I knew exactly what she meant. Soon we would be coming back to Haiti, back to Cecile, back to meet the children and begin whatever work was in store for us.

But there was more than that. It wasn't just a promise to Haiti—it was a promise to God. We were coming back to Him. We knew we were on the path that He had laid out for us, and nothing would stop us from moving along it, getting deeper and deeper into the adventure He had for us.

Marie filled the phone line with prayers of praise and delight, and I listened, nodding as more tears fell down my cheeks.

For so many years I had felt lost. I'd felt it in Haiti as a rebellious teenager and in New York as a fresh-faced immigrant. It had been there when I was in Florida trying to make it as a businesswoman but watching my plans and dreams sink without a trace. And I'd felt it in Charlotte when my marriage had crumbled and turned to dust before my own eyes. For years I'd not known where—or who—I was supposed to be. I'd failed as a mother, failed as a wife, and until I met Marie, I'd been convinced that even as a Christian I was weighed down by the shame of my past sins.

But not now. I finally felt like I knew where and who I was supposed to be. I had been looking in all the wrong places—in sex, in status, in relationships. I had been searching in the land of wealth and privilege, when all along I was supposed to be here, to be helping, to be trusting God for whatever He had in mind for me to do next. It was as simple as that.

"God," I prayed silently as my call with Marie ended and I looked through the window at the planes on the tarmac, "You said wherever I put my feet You would give me. So I'm claiming this land and that whole village for You."

PART TWO

5

SPEAKING TRUTH TO SIN

The Haiti of my childhood was so different from the Haiti to which God called me back. Some of the changes have been positive, but not many. Most of the transitions that my homeland has gone through have left people poorer, more fearful, and deeper in darkness.

My earliest memories of life in Port-au-Prince are of people. Everywhere I went, every moment of every day, people had been pressed in close beside me. Our three-room home had always been full of living, breathing, laughing, shouting, sweating, sleeping bodies. Besides my parents, there were my seven brothers and sisters, grandparents, and other relatives, plus the eight other children that my father had with other wives. They lived with us, too—both the children *and* the wives. We had no choice but to share everything. Food. Water. Blankets and clothes. The thin strip of floor on which we slept. The attention of our parents.

We hadn't lived in the worst part of Port-au-Prince—the infamous Cite Soleil slum—but what our area, Fort Nationale, lacked in violence, it more than made up for in overcrowding. Homes were packed so tight that, seen from above, Fort Nationale looks like it is made of armor, an infinite number of faded metal roofs pressed in on all sides. Thousands upon thousands of people live pressed in together on an area as densely packed as almost any slum in the world. There are barely any roads wide enough for a car to drive down, but the whole area is covered by a network of corridors only wide enough for two people to pass. They weave around the homes like capillaries on a medical scan.

But the crowding and the constant press of bodies and the lack of space were not a problem. They were an advantage. There was safety in numbers.

Every morning I'd pick up my white plastic one-gallon bucket and join the crowd of siblings and half siblings that left my home to fetch water. Before we took one step outside, we'd always check our feet. Nobody went barefoot. Ever. Not because we might tread on something sharp—though we might and sometimes did. The main reason we never left the house without either shoes or each other was simple—if we got caught by the authorities looking like we were poor and abandoned, we'd be snatched from the street by the government.

Our president, Papa Doc Duvalier, had a range of tools that he used to exercise his brutal control of the people. If members of his *bien-être social* (social well-being) office saw a young couple being affectionate as they walked down a street late at night, they would stop and question them. If the correct marriage papers were not produced, they would haul the couple off to get married right away.

While we did all we could to avoid the *bien-être social,* they didn't terrify us nearly half as much as their colleagues known as the *chalan.*

Not a child in the city wouldn't run away in terror when they saw the black sedans cruising the streets.

The *chalan* were on a mission to clear Port-au-Prince of street children. If they saw a child who looked lost, poor, and upset, who was walking barefoot or was just plain dirty, they would haul the child into the back seat just like the *bien-être social* did with the young couples. Only instead of ending up married, these street children were put in the care of social services. And everybody knew that was the worst thing possible. Nobody would hear from you again.

So I came to see that crowds provided safety. When we marched through the corridors of Font Nationale, swinging our empty buckets in a line as long as a bus, I felt good for the simple reason that I was not alone. I belonged. I was safe.

And I needed to feel safe. To my mind, it took forever to make our way out of the tightly packed housing and onto the street, but I always made sure that I checked off the markers that I'd memorized as I walked. I feared that if I lost my way, I would be lost forever. Part of me liked to be able to look up and see the sky, but like a deer emerging from a forest, we knew we were more vulnerable out in the relative space of the city.

When we reached the water tap and lined up, often for an hour or more, sometimes we'd see the kind of children that the *chalan* hunted. We called them *restavecs,* which in French means "stay with." These children had been sent by their families in the mountains to live with relatives in the city, often to help out with chores. We didn't pity them for their work—we all had to work—but we pitied them for being alone and lost and not knowing how to navigate their way back through the corridors to the homes they were staying in. Whenever we saw them sitting by the roadside, crying, we knew it was only a matter of time before they would find themselves in the back of a *chalan* car, heading off to who knows where.

. . . .

Two months after I traveled to Fonds Baillard with Telfort and met the old woman, the voodoo priest, and Cecile, I stood with Marie in the same broken-down shelter that served as both the schoolroom and the church. I fought back the urge to cry. It had been years since I'd worried about being taken by the *chalan,* but that same emotion started filling me up, threatening to force all the air from my lungs.

It was a Saturday afternoon, and the members of the church had gathered to meet us. We had only been there a few minutes, but already we realized that our warm smiles and loud *hellos* were not going to be returned.

We were talking with the pastor, a man who was a little younger than me. His eyes were narrowed, his jaw set, and he looked at both of us with nothing less than contempt. Though I'd never been this close to a *chalan* agent, I wondered if this was what it felt like the moment you were snatched.

Marie and I stood. An awkward silence settled before the pastor repeated what he had said the moment we arrived.

"We don't believe you are Christians."

Marie laughed. "Can you explain why, pastor?"

He cleared his throat, ready to spit out the words. "Look at your clothes."

"My clothes?"

"Yes," he said pointing to the khaki cargo shorts Marie had on. "Those are men's clothes. The Bible commands us not to dress like that."

He paused and looked at me.

"And you. Those jewels you're wearing are not correct. If you served God, you would dress more modestly."

In the silence, I could sense Marie trying to rein in her emotions and weigh her response. All I could do was look at the rest of the people who had gathered behind the pastor. The congregation looked tired and weak, and a dozen pairs of eyes looked anywhere but at us. They shuffled awkwardly, looking cold despite the heat of the midday sun.

It felt odd standing there like that. Marie and I were being treated like minor criminals, hauled out and placed on display for the pastor to assess and evaluate. How could that be when we had come to join in a God-given adventure?

I looked out at the blank stares and downcast eyes, and I could only think of one word. *Restavecs.*

That's what these people reminded me of. It was as if they were powerless against the pastor. They were like those lost boys and girls I used to pity whenever I saw them sitting down at the side of the road, ready to give up. Fear had stolen all their courage and purpose. They had no idea where to go. They needed help; they needed rescuing. But were they brave enough to accept it?

Since my first visit to the village, Telfort had returned three times. He'd delivered all the supplies that we'd bought in the city on the day I first visited, and he had made sure that Cecile was paid each month. He had also been able to take some rice, beans, spaghetti, and corn with him on his visits, and the school had started to do what almost every other school in Haiti does—feed the children one meal during the day.

The numbers of children attending had grown. A dozen new pupils had enrolled and paid their fees of $5 per term.

How can the church not see this is a good thing?

I chewed on the thought a little more.

How can they not be grateful?

And then some more…

How can they be so weak and blind? If it comes down to a choice between the pastor and me, how could they choose him?

Stop.

I caught myself. I exhaled, and the frustration and anger started to loosen their grip on me. I looked at the rocky ground beneath my feet and felt my shoulders grow heavy.

I was making the story about me. *My* generosity. *My* vision. *My* need to be thanked and seen as someone doing something important.

I prayed under my breath. "God, I'm sorry. That was wrong of me. I don't want to be that way. You're the only way out here. You're the only one who can rescue this situation."

Marie shifted her feet and locked her eyes on the pastor. I trusted her and I trusted God, but I was still sure that something dangerous was about to happen.

The moment she spoke, I braced for impact.

"The Lord says you cannot be living the way you are and make people believe something that you're not living out. You need to change your life."

The pastor looked as though he had lost half his blood in a single stroke. He wobbled on his feet a little, opened his mouth, and tried to speak a couple of times, then turned and left.

I looked back at the church members, expecting them to ask us to leave. But the opposite happened.

The eldest of the women spoke up. "Will you come and join us for church tomorrow?"

Marie and I both had the same look of surprise on our faces. "Of course," I said.

"Good. We would like you to lead the service."

Marie and I spent the rest of Saturday afternoon at a guesthouse nearby, talking and praying about Sunday's service. When the morning arrived and we drove back to the village, I was nervous. As the people arrived wearing their best clothes, carrying their own wooden stools and benches, I looked for the pastor. No sign of him.

The service went as planned, with me leading the people in some songs of worship and then Marie preaching. Not long after she began, the pastor arrived and sat alone in the back. I looked at him and then Marie, waiting for something to happen. But she carried on preaching, and he simply listened.

It was only at the end that he spoke, addressing everyone in the church at once. "I would like to get up and say a few words."

The murmur of disapproval from the congregation was impossible to ignore, but it didn't sit right with me. As soon as Marie and I made eye contact, I knew she felt the same way.

Marie looked around her and smiled. "If he has something to say, he should be allowed to say it."

Nobody protested when the pastor walked to the front of the church. They listened in perfect silence as he began.

"I have to confess that when you came here, I was not happy. I judged you. I looked at you with your clothes and hair, and I decided you were not Christians." He paused and glanced around him. "We all decided that you were not Christians. But when you spoke to me yesterday and told me that God knows about my life and how I need to change, I knew I needed to listen. You don't know me, and nobody knows my secret, but I believe He told you about my life. The woman I am living with is not my wife."

He looked surprised when Marie and I laughed. Neither of us meant any disrespect, and I knew that it took real courage to stand up and say what he just had. But the way we all saw it, this was a time to celebrate. Whenever a lost son turns his face home, the master picks up his robes and runs out to greet him.

The next morning Telfort drove out from Port-au-Prince and, along with Marie, we took the pastor and his wife—and their birth certificates—to the city hall. They were married right there.

. . . .

Marie and I could only stay a few days in Haiti, but our short trip was enough to teach me some valuable lessons. As I stood in the departure lounge once again, I was grateful to God for reminding me that He was in charge, that He was on the move, and that none of this was about me. It was all about Him. I needed to trust Him completely and not get my motives mixed, because as soon as I got back to Charlotte, I knew I would have to take a bold step. I had to tell my boss that I was leaving.

I was in my third year of teaching French and math to third graders, and it was hard to leave. The school was a prestigious public school that served an affluent neighborhood. It offered its kindergarten through middle schoolers a broad curriculum with six different languages, including Chinese and Japanese. No wonder people with money wanted their kids to go there. But while most of the kids were from wealthy families, the school ran a lottery, and two or three in each class came from the projects. Inevitably, I was the teacher they got sent to.

I liked it. I had nothing against teaching kids who came from affluent homes. But teaching a child who lived in poverty and who had already started to believe that life was bleak—well, that was a privilege. I loved being the person who chose to trust them and not see them as a failure. Even though they were young, I saw in their defiance and poor choices a mirror of myself. If God could turn my life around, I believed He could change theirs as well.

It wasn't just the kids whom I liked having contact with. Their parents had their own needs as well. A lot of them had already lost confidence and started to believe their child was no good. Once that happened, many of them stopped working with their kids. As with the families of the *restavecs* at the side of the road, these parents would simply give up.

Of all the kids who were sent to me, John was the worst. He was wiry, always moving. He struggled to focus, and when he got frustrated—which happened almost all the time—his anger could flare in a fraction of a second.

John had been thrown out of every first-grade class he entered. The school tried to encourage him by drawing up a behavior chart that could be filled in by each teacher at the end of every lesson. I got the feeling that seeing all the blocks colored in red only made things worse.

When he started coming to my French class, I decided to make him a leader. I gave him clear responsibilities and created as many opportunities as I could to praise him. Within two weeks, his behavior chart in my class showed nothing but green. It deserved a phone call home.

"You're from what?"

His mother couldn't hear me well, and I had to repeat myself, telling her that I was John's French and math teacher.

Before I'd finished I could hear her start to get mad.

"I thought this was going to be good with him in your class. I'm gonna kill him."

"No!" I almost shouted into the phone. "It's not that. I phoned because John has been doing so well in school, not badly."

She paused. "What did you say?" My words were clearly new and unfamiliar to her.

I explained again, telling her about John's leadership qualities and how he'd been well behaved for two whole weeks in my classes.

"I'm coming to see you."

A half hour later she was in my classroom, weeping. "I just can't believe it," she said. "I stopped hoping that John could ever be good in class."

It was difficult to leave pupils like John. I knew the challenges that Black kids faced, and I wanted to stay and help. I wanted to continue to be a voice speaking truth to John and all the other kids like him. I wanted to be someone who believed the best in them. I wanted to show that someone cared.

I wanted exactly the same thing for the children of Fonds Baillard. I knew I had to choose between them. The school in Charlotte had the financial resources that exceeded most of the other public schools in the district. They could pay for a new teacher. Fonds Baillard could not. If I did not answer the call and move to Fonds Baillard, who would?

Choosing to change my life so dramatically was simple, especially because I had not seen Michel for almost ten months. Instead of feeling abandoned or rejected by him, I chose to see the fact that my husband had walked out on me as a gift. I was free. It was my decision to make, and mine alone.

Marie and I talked about working together in Haiti, and though our plans were vague, I resigned soon after we flew back. I arranged to see out the school year and then move to Haiti in June. That gave me three months to make all the necessary arrangements, from ensuring I would be able to access my money in Haiti to giving away all the furniture and items that would not be getting packed into one of the three suitcases I was taking with me.

Each week I crossed another job off my list, but the closer I got to my one-way flight home, the more aware I was of one final emotion I had done nothing to prepare myself for. Fear.

I was about to move to an area I had not lived in before. I had no family in either the village or Fond Parisien, and by Haiti's standards that made me a complete stranger in the area. Not only did I not know anyone, I was unknown. That put me at risk. And being a woman on her own only made things worse.

I had money, but only a few thousand dollars. When that was gone, it was gone. I'd calculated that it would be enough to last me for four or five years, and I guessed that by then God would reveal the next steps He wanted me to take.

So, yes, I was feeling fearful. But I chose to let those worries about money and safety act as fuel for my prayers. Every time I was tempted to panic or stress about things, I got on my knees and remembered the prayer of an old British sea captain:

> Disturb us, Lord, when
> We are too pleased with ourselves,
> When our dreams have come true
> Because we dreamed too little,
> When we arrived safely
> Because we sailed too close to the shore.
>
> Disturb us, Lord, when
> With the abundance of things we possess
> We have lost our thirst
> For the waters of life;
> Having fallen in love with life,
> We have ceased to dream of eternity
> And in our efforts to build a new earth,
> We have allowed our vision
> Of the new Heaven to dim.
>
> Disturb us, Lord, to dare more boldly,
> To venture on wilder seas
> Where storms will show Your mastery;
> Where losing sight of land,
> We shall find the stars.
>
> We ask you to push back
> The horizons of our hopes;

And to push back the future
In strength, courage, hope, and love.

This we ask in the name of our Captain,
Who is Jesus Christ.

I wanted to risk everything for God. No holding back. No safety nets. Just me and Him and the adventure of a lifetime.

6

LIFE (AND DEATH TOO)

I cried every day during the first month I spent in Haiti. So many pupils had enrolled, and we now had over 120 pupils on our roll and only Cecile, myself, and two others to teach them. But I wasn't worried about the numbers. As I looked at them, crowded onto the benches Telfort had helped us make in the days before the term started, something deeper troubled me. Their poverty. That's what made me weep.

I knew the area well enough by now. I knew that few of the children could afford proper clothes, let alone shoes, and that a lot of the families were so poor that their children spent their days naked. I also knew Haitians value education highly, and no parent would ever want to show disrespect by sending a child wearing rags. Instead, they send their children wearing the very best clothes they possess.

The day the school opened, I got to see what their best looked like.

Junior wore a shirt so filthy it was impossible to tell what color it had once been. Angelo had on a pair of shoes so big he could only shuffle along in them. I thought that Edna was wearing a proper skirt at first until I realized it was an old feed sack. All of them were either dwarfed or squeezed tight by their clothes. None were clean. But all of them wore the same serious expression on their faces, desperate for this chance to learn.

It was those same faces that came to me when I was alone in the dark night. I'd picture them, and I would cry. No child should have to fight so hard to get an education. Did I really have what it would take to help them all?

* * * * * * * * * * * *

The first time I saw Ketna I found it impossible to hold back my tears. She staggered into the clearing in front of the school wearing a full-grown woman's heels and nightgown. She was seven years old and had likely never worn shoes before. What chance did she have in stilettos? She fell, and as I went to help her up, the air rang out with the sound of cruel laughter. I guess the other kids were relieved that someone was worse off than they were. To my American-trained eyes, they were all equally poor.

I had seen Ketna and her mother before, on the very first day that I had met Cecile. They lived in a shack beside the school. When Ketna fell for a second time, I looked over and saw that her mom was watching and calling her daughter to come back. She was crying too.

I got Ketna settled on a bench and went over to talk to her mom. She cried harder when she saw me approach.

"Do you have to turn her away?" she said.

"No!" I said. "She can stay. Of course she can."

She smiled a little with relief. "Her father said he was going to buy her some shoes and a dress so she could come to school. He promised, and she was so excited about it all. But it was a lie."

"She's welcome just the way she is," I said.

She hesitated. "What about the children laughing at her? Perhaps she is not ready and should wait until she has the right clothes."

I understood how she felt. I wanted to protect Ketna as well. But I knew that if she left now, she'd never return. "In life, it doesn't matter what people think. They will do what they're going to do no matter what. Leave her with me; let her come the way she is so she doesn't feel like she's not welcome here."

Her mother nodded, and I went back to the pupils. It was time to raise the flag, and as we gathered I called Ketna to come and stand at the front. She staggered on her heels, but by the time she made it to the flagpole—and the position of the greatest honor for any pupil during the ceremony—she had a smile as wide as the flag spread across her face.

After school that day, I took a tap-tap to Port-au-Prince and bought shoes for Ketna as well as for a few of the other pupils. I picked up some used clothes from street traders and balanced the large shopping bag on my lap as I made my way home.

Anyone who has ever been on a mission trip will know the blend of joy and chaos that was unleashed when I handed out the clothes the next day. And you'll know, too, the silent prayer I prayed—that these simple gifts might be multiplied, that the children might know for themselves the power and depth of the Father's love for them. *Jesus*, I prayed, *You took five loaves and two fish and fed thousands. Would You bless this offering of clothes and shoes so that these children might be filled with the dignity they deserve?*

. . . .

I decided I did not want anyone to feel inferior or superior in the school. Uniforms are a great leveler, and the clothes helped, but as the first week came to an end, another problem emerged. I noticed that the kids weren't all sitting down when the lessons began, and some were getting up and walking around midway through. When it happened on the first day, I didn't want to make a big deal of it. But by the time we reached Friday, a whole bunch of them were not engaging with the lessons.

I hadn't expected that. If you visit any other school in Haiti, you will find kids sitting down, eyes on the teacher, working hard every minute of the day. Even the very youngest ones know how important their education is. Schooling is a matter of life and death. You don't throw away something as important as that.

So why were my pupils switching off like this? Was there something wrong with the way I was teaching? Had my two decades in the U.S. created too big a gap between us? Had I offended some of them with the clothes and shoes I bought?

It turned out that the answer was none of the above. It was something far simpler.

During math I spotted one boy, JP, clutching his stomach. He was clearly in too much pain to concentrate on calculus, even though he was trying his hardest.

I waited until the rest of the class was busy working quietly, then crouched down beside him and asked, "When did you last eat, JP?"

His eyes filled with tears.

Later that night I finally was able to get through to Marie on the phone. "We've missed something," I told her. "These kids are so hungry they can't concentrate enough to learn. They need to eat, and we're the only ones who can feed them."

Marie did what she always does and listened quietly. I knew she was praying too. "Okay," she said eventually. "Leave it with me."

And so, the following Monday, right after we had given thanks to God through our prayers and worship, we ate Haitian peanut butter on yucca bread with wide grins fixed on our faces and gave thanks some more.

. . . .

In Matthew 25, we read the parable of the sheep and the goats. I don't know if I understand it fully even now, but I do know that putting clothes on the bodies of the naked and food in the bellies of the hungry is a good, good thing to do. There's no debate, no confusion. It's exactly what Jesus did.

Over the years there have been times when the smile of God has been missing from my life. I've found it hard to track down, and I've wondered what I've done that has caused this sense of distance between us. But right there, sitting among the peanutty faces and the hand-me-down clothes, I knew His presence. And I knew His pleasure too.

. . . .

I rented one room in a house in Fond Parisien. The other two bedrooms were rented by a woman who sold mangos and a man who worked as a doctor over the border in the Dominican Republic. Neither of them were ever there when I was. Each night I returned to the house and sat alone, splitting my time between preparing for the next day's lessons and trying to comprehend the depths of poverty in Fonds Baillard.

The Haiti of my childhood was a place of poverty, too, but a different sort. There were times when as many as 30 people could be crammed into our little home, but we always had enough to eat. Between the money my father earned as a stonemason and the weekly basket of oranges, avocados, sweet potatoes, and corn that my grandmother sent from her home in the mountains, we never went hungry.

In Fonds Baillard, almost everyone told me they were hungry. I tried encouraging people to grow their own vegetables, but the lack of rain made it almost impossible for anything to grow as fast as it did up in the mountains.

The only thing I could do was pray and trust that whatever needs were around me, God would meet them.

* * * * * * * * * * * *

I was alone in my room one Saturday morning when I heard someone calling for me outside. It was a woman, barely older than a child herself, with a little girl at her side, face buried in her mother's skirt. The school had been open for a couple of months, but I'd not met either of them before.

The woman didn't waste any time. "My daughter needs to see a doctor, but I have no money. Please, madame, will you help us?"

I looked carefully at the girl. There were no obvious signs of her being ill, but like her mom, she looked poor. "Okay," I said. "What's wrong?"

"She needs surgery. They tell me she has a tumor in her abdomen. Look." She carefully peeled the girl away from her leg and gently lifted the ragged T-shirt that was barely covering her. I hadn't been able to see it before, but now that she was standing on her own, the mass growing on her right side was clearly visible. It must have been about the size of my fist, and the skin was stretched tightly over it.

Either I helped her or I didn't. I did not take long to think it through. I had money, and I had no reason to doubt that they didn't. I also had nothing else to do that day. The choice was simple.

After we'd walked to the corner of the main street where the tap-taps congregated, I paid for the three of us to take a ride into Port-au-Prince.

My time as a nurse in America taught me the importance of good patient care, and I was impressed when the first hospital we arrived at saw the little girl right away and told us that in a few days there would be a free clinic run by American doctors. Removing benign tumors was one of their main activities, and assuming all the tests were good, they'd book the girl for surgery.

Two weeks later the little girl was back in the village, the tumor safely removed, the mom's smile restored, and my faith made stronger.

. . . .

A few months later another child was brought to me by anxious parents. This time it was an 18-month-old boy and I didn't need to ask to know what was wrong. He was hydrocephalic—the fluid on his brain had accumulated abnormally, putting pressure on his skull and causing his head to swell. I'd read about the condition before, but I was shocked by what I saw. The little boy's head was two or three times larger than it should have been.

His father and mother looked at me. They didn't need to tell me anything. I knew that I needed—and wanted—to help. I gave them enough money to get to the hospital and see a doctor, and I told them I'd be there after I finished teaching later in the afternoon.

I thought about the boy throughout the day. His situation appeared hopeless, but I reminded myself that God had the power to heal. Maybe He had the perfect doctor lined up, ready and waiting, just like He had when I met the young girl with the tumor.

. . . .

My phone rang as school was ending. I recognized the caller and considered dropping it. It was a man who had got my number by accident but who was now phoning me every few days to ask how things were going at the school in the village. I didn't know what his agenda was, and I didn't intend to find out.

I answered it all the same.

"You're calling again? What do you need, um…"

"Pierre-Richard. I thought it would be good to meet. I think I can help you with your work in Fonds Baillard."

I shooed away a stray dog that had come looking for scraps. "Well, right now the only kind of help I need is someone with a car. Can you help me with that?"

"A car? Sure. Where do you need to go?"

I was surprised he had a car, but I told him about the boy and how I wanted to go visit him in the hospital. We arranged to meet near my home where the tap-taps gathered, and I told him what I'd be wearing.

He didn't show up, so I called him. He picked up right away and sounded genuinely sorry.

"You said you'd be wearing a blue dress. I can't see anyone wearing that."

I could hear his voice in both my ears, so I turned around.

"Say that again, Pierre-Richard."

"What? I can't see anyone in a blue dress."

He was standing a few feet to my side, looking in the wrong direction.

"Well, I can see you. Turn around."

He spun, the wrong way at first, then saw me. I looked him up and down. He was well dressed, apart from the sandals. I was not impressed with the sandals.

"You've got a car here?"

He looked over my shoulders, scanning the crowds. "Yes," he said before turning to leave. "Just wait a minute."

It was all getting ridiculous, and I was seriously considering taking a tap-tap and going to the hospital on my own. But after a couple of minutes, a car pulled up in front of me, and Pierre-Richard jumped out of the passenger seat, holding the door for me.

I paused.

"This isn't your car, is it?"

He smiled. "No. But he'll take you to whichever hospital you need to go to. Isn't that what you need?"

All I wanted was to get to the hospital and see the family of the little boy, and to get there fast. There was a chance that the doctors might refuse to treat him if they didn't believe the family could pay for more than the initial consult. I climbed into the front seat while Pierre-Richard sat in the back. As we headed for the traffic of Port-au-Prince, I looked back in the mirror from time to time. His eyes looked sincere—kind—and I decided then that even though he was persistent and had bad taste in footwear, I could trust him.

. . . .

Things did not work out as I had hoped for the boy. He died the following Monday.

It rocked me. I had assumed God was at work and that somehow He was going to perform a miracle and save the boy. I struggled to understand what was going on. Had I failed? Had I heard

God wrong? Should I have gone with them myself to the hospital and left Cecile and the other teachers to cover my class?

I didn't know. And not knowing bothered me.

I was alone in my room one evening, thinking this over and getting nowhere, when I heard a voice I did not recognize calling my name outside.

I sighed.

I had forgotten to buy charcoal so had not been able to cook for myself that night. I was hungry and feeling low, and a part of me wanted to ignore the call. After all, God said He'd take care of me, and here I was feeling hungry and disappointed and not knowing how I was supposed to be helping. How could I go out and answer another call for help?

The voice called my name again. It was different from the voices that filled my day, and it took me a moment to work out why.

"Yvrose? You in there?"

It was an American accent.

I stepped outside and came face to face with a smiling young woman wearing a Chicago Bulls T-shirt.

"We're here on a mission trip, and we're staying next door. Do you want to join us for pizza?"

"Pizza?"

"Sure. It's not like it's deep dish or anything, but you're welcome to join us."

I laughed all the way to their house, and I couldn't stop smiling as I was introduced to the ten others who were visiting from her church.

Before I crammed the first slice into my mouth, I knew I needed to say something.

"I don't think it's good to waste time waiting to give your testimony, so I'm going to jump right in. I was at home just now, feeling confused and hungry. And now here I am sitting in front of all this food that God knew I wanted and needed. Thank you. You have made it possible for God to remind me that He is faithful to the last."

7

THE UNEXPECTED GIFT

As we approached the first anniversary of my move to Haiti, things were going well at the school. Our benches were full, word spread, and pupils had started coming from further away, some walking an hour to reach us each day. Watching them line up for the flag in the morning and then crowd onto our wooden benches in perfect silence as they listened to every word the teacher said filled my heart with joy.

I needed every last drop of that joy because as the first year in Haiti had progressed, I finally started to accept one of the most painful truths of my life—I was never going to have children.

It was so hard to accept, especially because when I'd left Charlotte I had been convinced that God was going to transform my barren life and give me the children I was desperate for.

The night before I had flown to Port-au-Prince a year earlier, I had been praying with friends when one of them stood up, his Bible open in his hand. "I've got this verse in my head that I can't get out," he said. "It's Psalm 113, verse 9."

Even before he could read it, I knew the words. One week before, another friend had phoned me up to tell me that she had been praying about me and wanted to share Psalm 113:9 with me.

"He gives the barren woman a home, making her the joyous mother of children."

At first it had been almost too much to take in. Like heavy rains after a drought, the words initially did not sink deeply into me. But, gradually, they did. Time and again I turned to the well-worn page in my Bible and read the words that shone like they were written in gold. Soon, I came around to the view that God was going to do something remarkable in my life.

I'd had a pretty good idea what that would be. At least, I'd thought I did. Since Michel and I were separated but not yet divorced, I assumed God would bring us back together and allow us to finally have a baby together. Since nobody in my family had ever divorced, it all made sense.

It was a beautiful thought. At times I could almost taste it. I was so convinced that this was what would happen that I even told Pierre-Richard. The day I'd first met him and we'd driven to Port-au-Prince, he'd asked me why I was in Haiti alone.

"Oh, I'm married all right," I said. "I'm just waiting for my husband to return."

Trouble was, I started to doubt that myself. From time to time I'd dream of Michel, but he was always either running away from me or ignoring me as I called out to him. One time I dreamed he was standing before me with a suitcase in his hand. When he turned and walked away, I knew it was forever.

. . . .

A little after my one-year anniversary in Haiti, I flew back to Charlotte. I did not plan on making it a long trip, and I only had one task to tick off. I returned to get a divorce.

The decision had taken a lot of praying, a lot of crying, and a lot of asking God what was going on. But to the best of my understanding, I was doing the right thing. For two years I had heard nothing from Michel. He had simply vanished off the face of the earth. I wasn't surprised, though. The last words he'd said to me were "You'll never hear from me again."

Even so, I spent my first week in North Carolina fasting and praying. *Dear God,* I pleaded, *if we are meant to live the rest of our lives together, then let me hear from him. But if it's never meant to happen, then let me never hear from him.*

I had sent letters to Michel at every address of every relative of his that I could remember, called every number I'd ever had for him, but I'd got nowhere.

North Carolina law allows couples who have been separated for one year to legally divorce. Michel and I had not lived together for two years, so I filed.

My first application was rejected, but after explaining to the judge that I was living in Haiti as a missionary and being granted a divorce would allow me freedom, I was told that I could collect my divorce papers.

A decade later, incidentally, Michel finally broke his promise. Without warning he called me one day.

"I'm sorry," he said.

It took me a moment to find the words, but I knew exactly what I needed to say. "Don't be sorry, Michel. I'm not. What you did put me in a better position."

We talked a little, but not for long. My life had changed so much since we were married, it was as if I was a different person. "Michel,"

I said as it was time to end the call, "it is for me to thank you. I never dreamed I'd be living this life. Don't feel bad about us."

* * * * * * * * * * * *

Within a few days of landing back in Haiti, Pierre-Richard phoned. We had become good friends, and he knew the reason for my visit to Charlotte. Even so, I was surprised when he asked me to marry him.

"Well, I want to talk to Marie first," I told him.

"Fine," he said. I could imagine his big, kind eyes shining. He sounded confident.

Marie was less so.

"I'm not getting any confirmation at all," she said. "I think God has someone for you to marry out in Haiti, but he's younger than you. You say Pierre-Richard is older, right?"

I'd had a conversation about age with Pierre-Richard not long after we'd met. I'd told him mine—I was about to turn 45—and he had laughed and told me that he was *waaaay* older. It was a weird conversation, and I was glad when we moved on. We'd never discussed our ages since then.

Marie's opinion mattered to me. I'd made enough mistakes in my life to know that I needed someone wise and prayerful on my side.

"Listen to me, Pierre-Richard," I said when I saw him next. "Marie didn't get any confirmation, and that matters to me. She's not sure God's in it, and the last thing I want to do is get married without being sure."

Again, he took it well. He smiled and told me he was going to pray about it.

Two weeks later the subject came up again, but not between Pierre-Richard and me. Marie phoned and sounded a little anxious.

"I need to apologize, Yvrose. I was praying, and the Lord told me that I was wrong for saying no about Pierre-Richard."

My heart quickened. "Really? How come?"

"He said He'd already shown me that you would marry someone you met out in Haiti, and he would be younger than you. I think that's Pierre-Richard."

"No, Marie, it can't be him. He says he's older than me."

Marie paused. "I don't think so. Let me talk to him."

It did not take long for them to figure it out. It was true that Pierre-Richard had told me he was older, but he explained that he only said it because he hadn't believed that I was 45 when we first talked about our ages. He figured that since I was joking about my age, he would too. The truth was—as Marie discovered—that he wasn't close to my age at all. He was ten years younger.

When Marie relayed all this to me after their conversation, it took me a while to process.

"But," I stammered, "he has some gray hair already. He can't be younger, can he?"

Marie laughed. "He's younger. And the Lord has showed me he's the one He prepared for you."

· · · · · · · · · · · ·

It was not hard to fall in love with Pierre-Richard. Our friendship was strong and built on a shared love of serving God side-by-side. We had worked closely together and kept our friendship pure, free from anything that would drag us down.

We both had our wounds. He had been engaged to a woman, but she got pregnant by another man. It caused him deep pain, and when he spoke about it, I could feel the sadness pressing on my chest.

But our wounds did not define us. I knew that Pierre-Richard would make a good companion. He was great with children and was easily the kindest man I'd ever met. He was always ready to give whatever he could to help. It was obvious that God had provided me with a good man to marry, so how could I say no?

Besides, I'd already used all his savings to pay teachers' wages.

Just one question remained in my mind. I could never give him children. Could he cope with that?

"I'm getting older," I told him. "For a while I thought I was going to have children, but I know now that I won't. Can you live without having a child of your own?"

Again, it was his eyes that spoke to me. Such kindness. Such love. Such care.

"Yes," he said simply. "Yes."

8

A KIND OF ENDING

Night falls quickly in Haiti. And when it does, the country is transformed. This darkness that settles across my homeland is about more than the lack of streetlights. It's spiritual as well as physical. When the sun sets and the moon rises, so many people in Haiti welcome evil. Through the practice of voodoo, they invite the devil himself into their homes and villages.

I have seen the effects of witchcraft on lives. I have stood face-to-face with people who have wished me harm. I have come closer to evil than I ever wanted. All these experiences taught me that we serve a greater power. They've reminded me that He who is in us is far, far greater than he who is in the world (1 John 4:4). But I'd be lying if I said I'd never been scared.

Shortly after Pierre-Richard and I were engaged, we spent a Saturday up in the mountains near Fonds Baillard, telling families about the school. Even though the cities have their slums, poverty in Haiti is often at its most extreme in the mountains. It can take hours to travel as little as one or two miles along steep, dangerous tracks that are only accessible by foot or donkey. The people who live in the cold air and thick forests are isolated, cut off from what little help and hope is in the rest of Haiti. The darkness that falls there is the darkest of all.

We met a mother who asked us to help her 17-year-old daughter, Estania. She had been sick for some time and was now weak and dehydrated. I agreed to take her back down the mountain and have her stay with me for a few days to get some fluids in her and try to rebuild her strength.

Late on Saturday night, Estania was sleeping in my room. As usual, the mango seller and the doctor were away, so Pierre-Richard was about to go to bed in one of the empty rooms. We were alone, talking about the kind of things that couples do when they have a wedding coming up.

Estania's shouting made both of us jump.

"I'm coming! I'm coming!"

There was something about her voice that made me run into her room, not walk.

She was still asleep, thrashing around on the bed. Neither of us could wake her at first, but when we finally were able to, she stared at me with blank eyes. She breathed rapidly and looked scared.

"It's okay, Estania," I soothed. "You're safe."

Her breathing calmed a little, but the fear remained. Pierre-Richard and I had been talking with her about Jesus earlier in the day, and I felt that this was the right time to return to the conversation.

"You know, Estania, Jesus can protect you from all harm. No matter what we're scared of, His love is enough to cast out all fear and bring perfect peace."

She closed her eyes and nodded.

"Would you like to say 'yes' to Jesus and follow Him like we talked about?"

She opened her eyes and nodded. "Yes."

The three of us prayed right there in the light of my and Pierre-Richard's cell phones. With tall shadows dancing on the walls, Estania gave her life to Jesus, received forgiveness, and confessed with her mouth that she would spend the rest of her life following Him.

She was asleep soon after, and Pierre-Richard and I went back to the living room to talk and give thanks, both too excited to sleep.

The shouting started an hour later.

It wasn't coming from Estania's room. It was coming from outside. It sounded like a group of men, and they weren't just shouting. They were chanting and banging drums as well.

I saw in Pierre-Richard's face a perfect mirror of what I felt.

Terror.

I couldn't hear what the men were saying, but I knew enough about voodoo to recognize the kind of rhythm and chanting used in witchcraft.

"We need to pray," Pierre-Richard said.

We were on our knees when I heard Estania come into the room.

"I know who they are," she said, her voice trembling. "I'm sorry."

"What do you mean?"

"They're called *bizango*. They're coming for me."

"Why?"

She started crying. "A friend and I were initiated into them. They made us do things. And tonight, I was supposed to bring them one person to prove myself to them."

The drums got louder. I looked at Pierre-Richard. His eyes were shut, and he was praying.

"I don't understand," I said. "Who were you supposed to bring to them?"

"Anyone," Estania whispered, crouching down on the floor beside Pierre-Richard and me. "It didn't matter. Whoever it was wouldn't come back."

"They'd be killed?"

"Yes."

Estania's panic grew. "Will Jesus protect me from them? I did bad things."

"He will," I said. "His blood is powerful. His forgiveness is enough to cover any sin. And His timing is perfect. That's why you're here tonight—so that you could give your life to Him and He could protect you."

The men outside were so close now, as if right outside our door. We all prayed, desperate for God to save us, pleading with Him to hold back the darkness filling the air outside.

As quickly as the *bizango* arrived, they left. But our prayers carried on until well past first light.

* * * * * * * * * * * *

Estania made a good recovery and continued to put her trust in God. That night strengthened my faith as well, reminding me of the threats we face as Christians and the importance of staying close to God. It also focused my thoughts on another night in 2002. A night when I had made a choice like Estania and turned toward the light.

I had been studying abroad in Spain. Life with Michel in North Carolina had been difficult, and the idea of spending four months away from him was appealing. I was hoping that it would give me time to escape the cycle of pain and miscarriages.

Soon after my arrival, I found out that I was pregnant. I was so happy. I told myself that being away from all the stress of life with Michel was going to make all the difference this time. Life in Spain would be calm and peaceful, and I could focus on my studies, living a healthy life. By the time I was finished studying, my first trimester would be over. I'd be out of the danger zone. Surely this time I'd carry the baby to term.

Halfway through my time in Spain, I had a doctor's appointment one morning. After an ultrasound, blood test, and other checks, I was told that everything looked great. I left the hospital feeling as though nothing in my life could extinguish the joy held within me.

But that same evening, I experienced the pain, the blood, the empty feeling within me that were all so familiar. For a moment I tried to convince myself that I was imagining it, that I was still pregnant and my hopes for the life growing inside me remained intact. But it was no use. I knew it was over.

The bleeding continued, so I went back to the same hospital I had skipped out of hours earlier. I walked through the doors feeling defeated. I was flesh and bones, blood and hair, but not much else. I had no joy. I barely had life.

I ended up on a hospital bed, alone.

The tears wouldn't stop. Questions stuck in my head like rusty fishing hooks. I didn't even want children, so why did I keep on getting pregnant and then losing the babies? Was God really still punishing me for my abortions? Or was I getting caught in the cross fire of a battle between God and the devil?

Whatever it was, I decided that I was done with it all.

"Go!" I whispered to the cold air. "Both of you! I want you both to leave me alone. Whatever there is between the two of you, leave my body alone. I don't want either of you in my life. Leave me."

As soon as the words left my mouth, I sensed the change. Even though it was bright in my room, I could feel the darkness growing. With each second that passed, I felt it get darker. It was like I'd closed my eyes, placed my hands over them, and turned off all the lights in the world. There was nothing but the dark.

Terror.

Out of nowhere I became aware of a new sensation as warmth and wet spread out across my sheets. I looked and saw I was bleeding again. I tried with all my strength to push the call button, but my arms would not respond. I was pinned down by an invisible force. I tried to open my mouth and shout for help, but no sound came.

"This is it," I thought. "This is how I die."

The darkness was everywhere, swallowing up everything in its path. I knew it soon would take me as well.

There was just one glimmer of hope within me. It was so faint I almost couldn't hold on to it, but I knew it was my only chance. Even though I'd just rejected Him, I called His name.

"Jesus!"

The darkness left as quickly as it had arrived. I could see the neon lights of the room again, and I could move. I edged myself out of bed and across the floor to the bathroom. By the time I reached it, a nurse came in. She gasped when she saw me.

"Why didn't you call?"

I could not explain why. But I knew that whatever had happened to me was over. And I knew the only way I would live my life was by trusting God.

"I have seen the darkness," I said to myself as I climbed back into the bed, "and I'm choosing the light. I'm better off with Jesus."

. . . .

Almost immediately after Pierre-Richard and I announced that we were getting engaged, the whispers started. Villagers complained that I was showing favoritism to one family over another, or that by getting married I was turning my back on the school. The closer we got to our wedding, the worse it became.

It drove me nuts, especially as the whispers stopped being shared in secret and started being broadcast in public. One day, when

Pierre-Richard and I were walking through the village, we overheard an old couple discuss us.

"They're taking all the money from the school!"

"Really?" I said, spinning around to confront the man and woman. "Is that what you think? Let me tell you the truth: I'm using my own account to run the school. That's my savings, my pension, and when it's gone, it's gone. And I'm using Pierre-Richard's money as well, and my brother Telfort's. I'm using everything I have, and very soon there's going to be nothing left!"

Neither of them said anything. I knew it wasn't the last time this would happen, and I knew their complaints weren't really about the accounts. Like a lot of the other villagers, they were upset because I had gotten wise to the trick they were playing and began to call them out.

It was Pierre-Richard who helped me see clearly. He opened my eyes to the way that a handful of people were playing the system by exaggerating their poverty. It was difficult for me to accept it at first. I wanted to believe the best in people, and I hoped that if I was generous and shared all I had, then others would do the same.

"Not everyone's like you," said Pierre-Richard. "Sometimes poverty makes people just as greedy as wealth."

A bitter pill to swallow, but I knew he was right. The more closely I looked, the more obvious it became that a few people were lying. They exaggerated how little they had, and they made up stories about sickness and urgent needs in order to stir my compassion.

I wasn't the only target.

As the school had grown, the church had grown too, so a few months earlier Pierre-Richard and I had helped to find a second pastor to help in the village. Luc was a good man and served God faithfully. He preached powerfully and was uncompromising when he taught about the need for holiness. A few of the villagers hated him for it, and they used witchcraft to try to kill him.

I was in Port-au-Prince one day, visiting my mom. Cecile called me and sounded anxious.

"What is it?" I asked.

"It's Luc. Nobody has seen him at all today. All his clothes are still in his room, but he's gone, and we don't know where. It doesn't feel right, Yvrose."

It was not typical of him to leave like that, and I phoned everyone I could think of. Nobody had heard from him. He'd just vanished.

I'd always been aware of the rumors that voodoo priests are able to make people vanish, but I'd never encountered it myself. Luc's disappearance had me worried.

I stepped out into the street and almost screamed with shock.

Luc was standing on the opposite side of the road, staring at me.

I ran over and grabbed his arm. I shook him for a moment, but he continued staring into space like a zombie.

I shouted at him. "Luc! Wake up!"

He blinked and his whole face changed, the way a child's shifts when they're suddenly woken out of a deep sleep. He looked confused at first, then scared. I told him everything was okay and guided him across the road into my mother's house.

When he'd drunk some water and sat down, he started searching for words.

"I couldn't…help it." He broke off and stared into space again for a while. "A voice told me to get up and go. I had no control. I just had to obey the voice."

A silence settled between us. I had no idea how he'd known where my mom lived. Was it a coincidence that I was there? Was he waiting for me? Was there a plan to cause me harm?

I shook the thoughts out of my head. "You need to go back to the village, Luc. Show them that you're okay."

He stared long and hard at me. "Those people are not serving God, Yvrose. They're serving other forces."

* * * * * * * * * * * *

I went back to the village that day. I could not sleep that night, nor the next. Pierre-Richard was working far up in the north, and he'd run out of minutes on his cell phone. So I sat alone in the evenings, reading my Bible by candlelight for hours at a time.

On the third night, I was starting to drift off to sleep as I sat with my Bible open on my lap. My head grew heavy and my eyes closed. I drifted. As I let sleep take over, I could hear the sound of a large crowd of people. At first it was just background noise, but the louder it became, the clearer it became. It was an army, and it was marching.

I woke up instantly.

The house was on fire. I checked my candle. It was still upright in the mug I had been holding all along. There was nothing nearby that it could have set light to. But on the other side of the room were boxes of stock cubes that we used for cooking the children's meals. Flames as big as my arm were dancing up the cardboard. I jumped to my feet and tried to put the fire out, but both arms of my pajamas caught fire.

My hands were in agony, and I was screaming. I ran outside and put the flames out in the dirt.

Neighbors came and put the fire out. Another fetched aloe from her garden and carefully split the spiny leaf, wiping the cool anesthetic all over my hands. I followed her to her house and fell asleep right away.

* * * * * * * * * * * *

No real evidence helped explain exactly what had happened, but together with what happened to Luc, I concluded that there was serious spiritual opposition to what we were doing there in Fonds Baillard.

I prayed hard about it all. I needed wisdom most of all and knew that the only source that mattered was God Himself. Almost as soon as I started to pray, I sensed that I needed to look closely at the little building we shared with the church.

I went as soon as I could and searched. What I found made me stop dead.

A piece of bread. A magnet. Needles. None of the things I found were unusual or mysterious on their own, but voodoo is a strange religion. Priests takes everyday objects and arrange them in precise ways to affect certain spells.

One look at the collection at the school was all I needed to know that someone had been practicing voodoo there. What I did not know for sure was whether they were doing it to attack the school or the church.

I found the pastor—not Luc, but the pastor whom Marie and I had met that first weekend we visited together. I held out the artifacts to him. "Do you know anything about these?"

He looked faint. "Oh, no, no, no," he stuttered. "But some people have asked me to do things like this for them."

I didn't bother waiting to find out whether he had helped them or turned them away. I couldn't trust him either way. Between him and the rest of the villagers who were working against me, I had more than enough understanding of what was going on. All I needed to know was what God wanted me to do about it.

. . . .

Pierre-Richard and I married soon after all this happened, and the tensions continued between us and the handful of villagers who were against us. It was easier to face their gossip and slander knowing that I had a good, prayerful, loving man at home, and I no longer felt so alone and vulnerable. But something had changed in my attitude toward the village, and I prayed desperately for God to show me the way out.

I spent many days praying and fasting until my eyes fell on a passage of Scripture that shouted loud at me:

> But if a town refuses to welcome you, go out into its streets and say, "We wipe even the dust of your town from our feet to show that we have abandoned you to your fate. And know this—the Kingdom of God is near!" (Luke 10:10-11 NLT).

I read those words of Jesus and felt as though He was speaking them directly to me. It started me thinking that it was time to go. But God knew in order to make such a big decision, I needed more than a hunch, so He coordinated events in such a way that I knew beyond doubt what I had to do next: I ran out of money.

My retirement fund which I hoped was going to last four or five years had barely made it 24 months. Pierre-Richard and I both knew that at some point soon I would have to return to the U.S. for a few months to earn some more money.

The only question was what would happen after I'd replenished my bank account. I knew that any trip to the U.S. would be temporary. But where would we end up in Haiti?

We both prayed and fasted, but no clear plan was revealed to us. We searched the Scriptures and talked late into the night. We talked with Marie and asked her advice. Nothing came of it. It wasn't easy to be unsure like that, especially as people continued to spread gossip and lies about us both. But we both believed that leaving was still the right thing to do.

• • • • • • • • • • • •

As we approached the end of my third year in Haiti, Pierre-Richard and I said goodbye to the school in Fonds Baillard and prepared to say goodbye to each other.

I had found a job looking after an elderly couple in Nantucket, but Pierre-Richard had been unable to get a visa to join me in the U.S. He didn't mind so much, as the idea of living in the U.S. never appealed to him. His plan was to return to Port-au-Prince and pursue some business opportunities. Being separated so early on in our marriage wasn't easy, but again, it was right. We knew if ever we felt unsure or troubled, all we had to do was remind ourselves of the ways in which God had been with us so far. He had brought us together despite the obstacles in our path. He had protected us from attack after attack. He had made a way for us and had never let us down. And He had revealed enough of the path ahead to know that soon we would be together again in Haiti, starting a new school and a fresh adventure with Him.

The day we said goodbye at the airport and I flew to the U.S., I told myself over and over that this was only temporary, that God had us in His hands, and that I could trust Him completely. He was the one who had given me those dreams about the mountain and the lake and the little children living in poverty. He was the one who had called me to Haiti, and He was the one who had given me my task to carry out. It was my burden to bear, my duty to fulfill. It was a privilege that I did not want to let out of my grasp.

PART THREE

9

THE DAY THE EARTH SHOOK EVERYTHING APART

Port-au-Prince, Haiti. Tuesday, January 12, 2010. 12:32 p.m.

Waiting in line to leave the airport, I knew exactly what was coming. At least, I thought I did. I could hear the chaos waiting for me on the other side of immigration. Not shouting or anger or anything like that. Just the chaos of people hustling for a living. The usual white noise of Haiti.

Once through the airport doors, I was careful to keep a close eye on my cases and not let any of the porters get their hands on them. If that happened they'd attach themselves to me and my luggage, not letting either of us go without my paying a substantial fee. Typically, I didn't mind paying. But this time I just wanted to get out and meet up with Pierre-Richard as soon as possible. After six months without seeing each other, I just wanted to hold him and be held.

After three failed attempts, I finally got through to him on his cell.

"I'm going to be late," he said.

"Traffic?"

"The car broke. Someone's fixing it for me now."

"Okay. I love you."

"I love you too."

Whatever chaos consumed the airport was nothing compared to what I could imagine on the roads outside. The traffic in Port-au-Prince can lock down at any time, day or night. Anything can cause it, from roadwork to traffic accidents, flooding, or even a single skinny-hipped cow wandering onto the road. The cause doesn't matter, and the effect is always the same. Within minutes the standstill begins to spread out, the roads turning to frozen arteries of a heart that has stopped beating.

Haitians are resourceful people, however. I broke free from the crush of the porters and made my way outside. I found a motorbike taxi who would take me, my backpack, and my large suitcase squeezed between us across the city to a hotel near my mother-in-law's house. Once I'd checked in, I went out for a stroll to kill time before Pierre-Richard met me at a local restaurant. I needed some space.

After six months of looking after one elderly couple in the calm of their 4,000-square-foot home in Nantucket, Haiti's people and sounds were calling to me. I wanted to be outside walking through the city. Moving was better than sitting still.

So I walked. I didn't know where I was going or how long until I would get there. I was just enjoying the air filled with smells of charcoal fires, the streets full of tap-taps loaded with people, the sidewalks overflowing with people selling everything and anything. It was chaos, but it was good chaos.

Soon I was near a part of the city that I remembered well from my childhood. The Presidential Palace was still here, looking the way I remembered it—splayed out wide across its perfect lawns like an ancient emperor reclining after a banquet. Every day when I'd go fetch water, I would pass by. And every time I was struggling to make my way home with my little white bucket, trying desperately not to spill any water, I'd pause outside the palace and stare.

There were other impressive buildings in the city, but none quite like this. I could hardly believe that any building could be so large. I had a favorite daydream that I often slipped into as I stood in front of the iron railings. I pictured the heavy gates swinging open and a shiny black car driving out. It would pause right beside me, and I would try to stare inside the blacked-out windows. Eventually, one of the windows would wind down and I'd see him, the president.

"You are working hard and you're very strong," he'd say, looking at me and all the other kids gathered around. "Come into the palace. You've earned it."

My daydream never got as far as us actually getting inside the palace. But that didn't matter to me. Maybe all I needed then was the idea that someone with the power to change things had actually recognized me. And as I'd pick up my bucket and begin my slow journey back home, I'd often long for the day when I didn't have to go so far to collect water.

· · · · · · · · · · · ·

In many ways, not much had changed in the four decades that had passed. Staring at the palace in January 2010, I felt just as restless as I did when a child. I had the same feeling that something needed to change in my life, and I still needed someone powerful to change it. The only difference was that at least now I knew it wasn't the president to whom I should be looking. The only one whose help I wanted was God's.

And I wanted His help more than ever.

The six months in Nantucket had been good, though they had included two unexpected surprises. I hadn't predicted how hard it would be to reintegrate myself into life in one of the world's wealthiest countries. I tried to be normal and do the things that I used to when living in Charlotte, but going out and spending $20 on a meal was no longer a pleasure. Almost every time I looked at a menu, I would calculate how many children in Fonds Baillard I'd be able to feed for the price of a bowl of clam chowder or fillet of sea bass. It was hard enough to visit a mall, let alone a shoe store. The more I tried to do the normal American things, the worse I felt—as if all my taste buds for wealthy, comfortable living had died through lack of use.

Then there had been the money. I started the job on an agreed $300 each week. I knew it was low for a nursing assistant, but I had calculated that it was enough for me to live on and save a couple of thousand dollars to bring home. Halfway through my contract, something happened that changed everything, though. The family of the couple I was caring for increased my weekly wages to $1,250. I was grateful, of course, but it went deeper than that. Pretty soon I began wondering if this was God's way of sending me down a new path. It felt like an opportunity to raise more money and do even more good back in Haiti.

As I'd prepared to return to Haiti in January, restlessness grew within me. My plan looked good on paper, but something about it didn't sit right within me. I prayed, fasted, and talked to many different people in Nantucket, but the restlessness remained.

The best advice I'd received was from my pastor at the little church in Nantucket. "God is a great provider," he said one Sunday as I helped him stack chairs after church. "If He wants you back in Haiti, He'll make a way."

Counting down the days to my departure, I'd prayed and fasted all the more. I was pleading with God to reveal His plans to me. Where did He want me to go in Haiti? Who did He want me to help?

When no clear answer came, I did what Christians have been doing for generations. I made my own plan.

My sister lived in Port-au-Prince, and like everyone in my family, she had a heart for the children everyone else overlooked. She had opened her home to several children living on the streets, and I had been supporting her for a while. I helped fund a teacher and set up a small school near my sister's house that educates the children she had taken in as well as others who could not afford to pay school fees.

My plan was to do more. A lot more. Friends from Nantucket had already sent me an old tarpaulin. I was going to find some more land and create a bigger school that could take in more children. If I based myself in Nantucket and traveled back every few weeks, I'd be able to do so much more in Port-au-Prince than I had in Fonds Baillard. I knew that I could live cheaply and figured that with a budget of more than $3,500 each month, I could help hundreds of children.

It was a good plan and I had it all worked out, so why did I still feel restless? I was back in Haiti, but was I where God wanted? These were questions that I couldn't answer, no matter how long I stared at the Presidential Palace and prayed.

Pierre-Richard called. The traffic was easing, and he would be at his mother's house before long. We traded *I love you*s and ended the call. I turned my back on the palace and started the long walk back to my mother-in-law's house.

Before I was halfway there, the earth began to shake.

• • • • • • • • • • • •

Port-au-Prince, Haiti. Tuesday, January 13, 2010. 5:21 a.m.

After we had been reunited and dried our tears, Pierre-Richard and I had worked side by side all night, only returning to his mom's house when the sky began to lighten. Neither of us could sleep, so I took a few moments and sat in the yard, leaning against a wall. I closed my eyes and ignored the taste of dust in my mouth. After helping on the streets all night, my mind was full of images. Ghostly-looking rescuers desperately clawing at the bases of buildings folded flat on themselves. Bodies laid out across the rubble. The young pregnant woman, her face contorted with agony as she battled for her final breaths.

Cell phone service was still down, but I had heard news from some of my family already. My mom's neighborhood had escaped the worst of the earthquake, and Telfort and Pastor Jean had both been out of town. Still I'd heard nothing from my sister. As soon as the sun started to rise, Pierre-Richard and I made our way toward her.

Morning's dawn did not bring the hope of a new day. It only intensified the suffering of the previous one. Out on the streets, death was everywhere—if anything it felt closer than it had in the night. For each survivor pulled from the rubble, many more life-less bodies were laid on the ground. We helped where we could, but with every minute that passed, I felt the pull to be with my sister.

She was in the yard outside when we reached her, her house nothing but rubble and dust.

"We lost six students," she said quietly. "And a teacher. She was pregnant."

We embraced. I was the one who melted. I was no longer an adult a couple of years away from her fiftieth birthday. I was a child again, hoping to lose my fear in the arms of her big sister. Heavy sobs poured out of me.

When I had recovered my breath a little, she took me to the churchyard where she ran the school. Like the school in Fonds Baillard, it had been nothing more than an open space with a tarpaulin roof. But it was destroyed. The surrounding buildings had collapsed, filling the yard with rubble. To the side lay the bodies of those they had pulled out from beneath the concrete. They were covered with the tarpaulin.

I stared for the longest time.

I'd seen death before, and I could easily remember children from Fonds Baillard who had died. This was different. Seeing the little bodies lined up like that changed me—it couldn't *not* change me. An ache more powerful than any I had ever known opened up deep within me.

. . . .

Over the following days, Pierre-Richard and I worked in the neighborhood. We started by using the tarp we had sent to my sister. Instead of using it to expand the school, we created a shelter for her and her family to sleep under. When she met others who had lost their homes, my sister invited them to share her space. Within a couple of nights, eight families crammed under the heavy-duty plastic sheeting.

In the days immediately following the earthquake, there was no sign of the UN in the area. The government appeared to have vanished too. While food and water were still for sale around the city, there was no organized system for distributing it. People who were too sick or injured to travel across the city to buy supplies were left with nothing. Within days we heard stories of people dying because they could not access the treatment they needed.

Using the money that I had brought with me from working in the U.S., Pierre-Richard and I traveled to the stores we heard were still standing. We bought as many basic supplies as we could—rice, oil, charcoal, water. We then filled the van with people from the church and drove around my sister's neighborhood, distributing what we'd bought. Working as a large team, we were able to support hundreds of people in that first week.

It was hard work, and barely an hour went by without our being reminded of the overwhelming scale of the task ahead. The further we traveled throughout the city, the more devastation we saw. Even working with the others, we were too small to make a dent in the suffering that the earthquake created. And yet, there was something almost satisfying about those days. The restlessness I had been feeling for weeks vanished. In its place came a deep knowledge that this was where I needed to be.

. . . .

It took almost a week for something else to dawn on me. I was in the middle of a turning point in my life.

At first, I thought my feelings were simply a case of survivor's guilt. In the occasional moments of calm that I experienced each day, my mind would cut back to the earthquake. The memories were so vivid that I could almost feel the earth shaking beneath me, almost hear the sound of tumbling concrete and the piercing screams of people caught up in the terror. The earth threw me from one side of the street to the other, always just in time to spare my life as another building came crashing down. People whom I had been standing next to one minute were dead the next. I had no control and could only reach one conclusion: The way my life was spared was nothing less than a miracle. I knew there was no way I should have survived that day. It was not enough to simply acknowledge this and say thank you. There had to be an answer to the question, *why?*

For months I had been asking what God would have me do, and solving that particular puzzle had felt like an all-out impossibility. But here in Port-au-Prince, with dust in my eyes and hunger pains in my belly, the answer presented itself with almost perfect clarity. Why had God spared me? With every bone and muscle inside, I knew.

That moment of being completely powerless during the earthquake was the key. I had been like a puppet, unable to save myself. I only survived because the hand holding the strings wanted me to.

It had been years since I looked at God that way.

He had saved me because He was not finished with me. And He had saved me because I needed to change. I could not go on the same way anymore. For so long I had been controlling things.

I can't tell you how I was able to arrive at these conclusions. No bright light appeared or voice from the clouds spoke. There weren't even any conversations where someone carefully explained it all to me. I just knew. The same way you know that when you next inhale there will be oxygen to fill your lungs, I knew this fresh perspective was true.

As the dust from the earthquake finally settled, so too did the fog in my mind. Finally, I had a clear perspective, one that I felt I'd been lacking for years. At last I could see how far I had walked away from the path God had laid out for me.

The problem was that I had taken control. I had made the work in Fonds Baillard about me. I had allowed my ego to take over.

Like so many people, I had started out with good intentions. Ever since I first arrived in Haiti almost four years earlier, I had been aware of my responsibility to serve God faithfully. Having received all those dreams, and then arriving at Fonds Baillard and seeing the exact same location and people, had blown my mind. I hadn't really believed that God could speak so directly to people. And because this was so new and unexpected, a part of me started to believe that I was special.

I had a lot of flesh in my work for God. I wanted to do well, and I wanted to do well in my own strength. The way I saw it, God had given me the unique calling as well as all the resources I needed. This was my task to fulfill, my burden to shoulder. Even though I would never have admitted it at the time, I believed God called me to do it, so I was going to be the one who should be doing it.

This led to some bad choices.

When someone criticized me for not making the school in the village look more like a school—with better benches, better resources, and so on—I hardened my heart toward them and decided that I would not ask them for any more help again, ever. I rationalized it as an opportunity to show God how committed I was to doing it all on my own.

When one of the churches in the U.S. that had been supporting us financially called me out for not having proper procedures in place for showing how the work was making a positive impact, I withdrew from them too.

From then on, I didn't turn away help, but I did not tell people what I was doing. I did not share the story of the work in Fonds Baillard. I kept it secret. I was jealous and wanted to keep it to myself.

What hurt most was feeling like I was on my own. Yes, Pierre-Richard was with me, and Telfort and Pastor Jean had both worked hard to support the work in so many different ways, but even those three men, whom I trusted with my life, I didn't trust completely with the work. It was my vision, my burden, my baby.

What hurt most was the knowledge that it had almost been so

different. When Marie and I first visited the village and shared that incredible weekend when the pastor married his partner, we had both talked about moving to Haiti together. It was going to be the two of us working side by side in Fonds Baillard. But Marie hadn't come. I understood why, and none of what followed was her fault. We spoke on the phone regularly, and Marie walked the journey with me in prayer and always gave financially to the work. Now we talk every day, and her staying in the U.S. is unquestionably the right thing. The problem in those early days was how I responded to the gap that she left behind. Instead of leaning heavily on God, I loaded yet more of the burden onto my own shoulders.

I also allowed the first crack of doubt to grow. Why would God call both of us to Fonds Baillard, and then I was the only one going? I shed a lot of tears over that question and spent a lot of time wondering if maybe God didn't send me after all. Maybe I came by myself. Maybe I didn't see those dreams. Maybe I made it all up.

God is so kind. Whenever I sank into moments of doubt and fear like this, the next day someone would call and give me something that I needed—food or money, reassurance, encouragement or prayer. This happened a lot during those early years. But even so, as I was finally able to view my life with clarity in the wake of the earthquake, I had to admit that part of me had begun to grow resentful of God.

Haven't I shown faith? Haven't I been a faithful servant by leaving the U.S. and coming here to serve You? Haven't I done enough?

I whispered these questions to God, knowing already that the answer would sting. And sting it did.

God showed me the truth about how stuck up I had become. It wasn't faithful service that I'd been offering. It had been my ego, my flesh, and my fear driving me. That was why I returned to the U.S. for half a year once my money ran out. I trusted myself more than I trusted Him.

The revelation that finally took the air from my lungs and left me sobbing on the ground was this: I had become the mule that Michel's girlfriend had called me. From the moment she'd taunted me with it, the word *mule* felt like a curse. Finally, I could see that I had taken it on, absorbed it deep within me. All I was good for was work. I was a mule. I was a beast. It was how Michel had seen me, and somehow, part of me had believed it was how God saw me too.

* * * * * * * * * * * *

Ten days after the earthquake, I sat with Pierre-Richard on the pile of rubble that used to be my sister's house. He looked tired, and I knew I did too. But I could feel a new energy flowing through me. For the first time that I could remember, I felt free—no burden on my shoulders.

"Do you remember the piece of land you bought me when we got engaged?"

Pierre-Richard looked awkward, and I knew why. As an engagement present, Pierre-Richard had bought me a piece of land outside Fond Parisien. It was not much bigger than an eighth of an acre, but it had a view of the lake and was near a big house with a water pump. He'd bought it with a vague idea that one day we might build a house there. It was two miles away from the village, and he said that he thought it would make a great place to live.

When everything started to go wrong with Fonds Baillard, those plans had been killed off. I had said more than once that I was never going back to Fonds Baillard, and we both knew I would therefore never want to live on the land he'd so kindly given me.

"It's okay," I said, smiling at Pierre-Richard. "Something good has happened."

He relaxed a little and looked interested. "What?"

"I've been thinking and praying, and I'm wondering whether

God might be calling us back to Fond Parisien after all. Do you think that maybe we could have the school right there on the land?"

Pierre-Richard's eyes smiled. "What about working in Nantucket to raise money? Do you still think you should do that?"

I shook my head. Deep in my heart I knew this was not the right plan. I had a job to do in Haiti, a God-given calling here to do His work and get my own hands dirty. He had given me so many dreams of that little corner of this country, and His invitation for me to follow Him here hadn't changed. If I chose to return to the U.S. and watch my bank balance balloon, I knew I would feel like I'd failed. I knew I wasn't called to be a philanthropist, supporting Haiti from afar.

"Good," he said. "I never wanted to spend time in the U.S. anyway."

. . . .

In the following days we both prayed and fasted. Soon we felt clear about what would happen next. The village itself was two miles away from the land in Fond Parisien. In most other countries, this would be too close, but in rural Haiti where people often live and work within a small area, two miles was plenty. We would be far enough away from Fonds Baillard but still able to travel into the mountains and continue the outreach we had begun to families like Estania's.

It wouldn't be easy, though. There were no buildings on the land, which meant that Pierre-Richard would have to buy a tarp and build our own simple schoolroom. We both liked the idea of starting small. It was simple, uncomplicated, and, best of all, it felt like we could trust God completely.

The land had been a gift. I had not earned it; I had simply been given it by a man who loved me unconditionally.

This fresh start felt exactly the same. Whatever this school became, whether it stayed small or grew large, I decided it was fine. It was not up to me anyway. Finally, I began to understand that none of this was about my work or my effort. It was all about God's grace and kindness.

10

BECOMING MAMA

Hurricanes have names, but earthquakes are known by their numbers. I don't think the numbers from the 2010 earthquake will ever be far from my mind: 7.0 magnitude; 250,000 lives lost; 300,000 injured; 5 million people displaced.

It was the greatest humanitarian disaster in Haiti's history. As images of the devastation spread across the globe, people responded, their compassion leading them to generosity. Within weeks we received a shipping container from the community in Nantucket containing tons of clothing, food, and emergency supplies like tarps and rope. Within days we had given it all away.

Pierre-Richard and I slept under the tarp at my sister's house along with eight other families. We spent our days working frantically, not only giving away what others had sent us, but also giving away everything that was ours to give. Our clothes, our money, our sweat, and our time. We gave it freely, not counting the cost.

Though we were surrounded by heartbreak and sorrow, and we had never been this close to so much death and grief, we knew without question that we were exactly where God wanted us. How did we know? Because of one more number that will forever tell the story of the earthquake's impact.

Twenty-one.

That's the number of children who came to us asking for help.

They didn't just want food and water. They wanted a home. And they wanted to come with us to Fond Parisien.

An 11-year-old boy called Luckmane was the first. I knew him already because he was one of the children enrolled in the school I had helped my sister start in Port-au-Prince. Luckmane was a bright, studious, and hardworking kid from Sous Terrace, a place almost as dangerous as the infamous Cite Soleil slum. He had told my sister that he wanted to go to school, but his father could not afford the fees. I'd sponsored him anonymously since then.

Luckmane was such a cute little boy. He was always ready to do whatever he was asked—always with a smile on his face. After the earthquake I asked everyone I could think of, but nobody had seen him. Days stretched by, and although I visited all the places I thought he might be, there was no sign of him. I hated returning to the tarp at the end of each day wondering whether he'd survived. I'd seen so many bodies, but the thought of him lying dead cut me.

My sister greeted us one afternoon as Pierre-Richard and I returned from distributing clothes and food.

"You need to come," she told me. "Luckmane's here."

She looked serious. I wanted to ask every question that was shouting out in my mind but held off and followed her to the tarp where Luckmane was sitting quietly on a pile of rubble. He looked just as serious as my sister.

I hugged him and felt my tears wash over my face. "Are you okay? What happened?"

Luckmane ignored my questions. "I want to come with you, Mama."

A volcano erupted within me.

I looked over at Pierre-Richard. He was crying harder than I.

"Of course," I said. "Of course you can."

. . . .

Saying yes to Luckmane opened the doors to so many others. Within a few weeks we had 20 other pupils from the little school in Port-au-Prince ask us to take them in. Some had been made homeless by the earthquake. Some had been made orphans. We explained to all of them that life in Fond Parisien was not going to be easy—we would be living under a tarp far away from the communities they had grown up in—but they all said they didn't mind.

In a lot of ways, I was stunned. I wasn't expecting anything like this to happen, but there were so many of these children needing our help that I could not ignore them. And the sense that God was doing a new thing in me had been growing since the earthquake, glowing warmer than ever in my chest. I knew saying yes to these children, no matter how long they ended up staying with Pierre-Richard and me, was a God-given invitation I did not want to ignore.

So we moved. Less than one month after the earthquake, 23 of us crammed into two tap-taps and one van and drove east. Pierre-Richard had already set up the tarp, and beneath it he had pitched some small tents that we had been given. I shared a tent with the girls, and Pierre-Richard was with the younger boys.

I looked at our sleeping arrangements that first night. Pierre-Richard had bought the land hoping to one day build a house for us. Now he was sharing a tent with a dozen boys. "Are you okay with this?"

Those eyes smiled again.

"But don't you feel like you should have your own children? How can this match up to that?"

He paused a while before responding. When he spoke, I knew the words came from the deepest part of his heart. "But Yvrose," he said, "these ones are handpicked by God."

. . . .

I heard someone say once that God's plans always have a birth, a death, and a resurrection. I suppose that is true, although in my case, even before I became aware of God's plan for me as a mother, there was death. A death so painful that it took the next three decades for the wounds to heal.

Moïka, the daughter I gave birth to when I was 17, was born with a white residue on her mouth. It was still there after one week and had not reduced as the end of her second week approached. I had tried not to stress about it, but in the end, I took her to the doctor. He waved his hand and told me it was nothing to worry about. After I'd paid his fee, he sold me some homeopathic medicine and told me to place it on her tongue.

I did exactly as I was told, carefully measuring out the precise amount that the doctor had prescribed. I had no idea that the medicine was never supposed to be given neatly like that.

I had no idea that it was always supposed to be diluted.

I had no idea that as Moïka stared at me with eyes wide open and swallowed, she was about to take her final breaths.

She died in my arms. Her eyes were wide open, locked onto mine.

. . . .

The memories of that day—Moïka's stare, her stillness, the way her tiny body grew so cold so fast—brought with them pain so great that there were times when I thought I would never breathe again. An agony that lasted for years. A pain that I wanted both to flee from and return to again and again—because each time I miscarried I thought that I was being punished for the abortions I had. I had killed my babies, and I deserved to be taken back to the pain of losing Moïka.

Over the years there were times when I tried to break free from this cycle of shame and pain, like the night in Spain when I turned my back on God completely. Another time I lit 12 candles—one for each miscarriage I'd suffered. "These are the babies I lost," I prayed out loud in the flickering darkness. "And Jesus, I never had closure. I know I have done some terrible things, but I'm giving this to You. I'm burying this pain that keeps on plaguing me."

I blew out the candles, took them outside, and buried them.

I never got pregnant again, but the pain remained inside.

* * * * * * * * * * * *

God gives, and He takes away. Slowly, our family of 21 children living under the tarp in Fond Parisien got smaller. Over the months that followed the earthquake, the children Pierre-Richard and I had found on the streets of Port-au-Prince left us. Some went to live with family members in the mountains; others returned to the city. Some discovered that their parents, whom they believed had died in the earthquake, were still alive. These were bittersweet moments. They were times to be thankful for the way God was putting families back together, thankful for the opportunity that God had given us to share our lives and our home with these children. But saying goodbye to them reawakened the familiar pain I'd been experiencing for years.

I knew that the hardest goodbye of all would be the last one I would have to say. It was only right that Luckmane should be the one child who we were left with—after all, he had been the first one in. But as we prepared to take him back to Port-au-Prince one Sunday so that he could be reunited with his father, I felt like I wanted the earth to stop revolving and never start again.

We had arranged to meet at the church where I had helped set up a school. Like every building in the neighborhood, it was broken, a large crack running across the front. The church wasn't anywhere near safe by American standards, yet we walked inside and joined the other hundred people who were squeezing themselves onto the wooden benches.

I found it hard to concentrate on any part of that morning's service. I wanted to sweep up Luckmane into my arms and run the 30 miles all the way back to Fond Parisien. I wanted never to return to this place, never to have to say goodbye to any child again. I dreaded the fact that within a few hours Pierre-Richard and I would walk onto our little plot of land, just the two of us, and sit alone beneath the tarp. We would be childless again. I couldn't bear it.

Every minute felt like torture, and I dreaded each tick of the clock that brought me closer to the moment when I would have to say goodbye. A couple hours later, the service was over.

Luckmane's father had entered the rear of the church with a little girl and an older boy. My sister saw him and crouched down, talking to Luckmane.

"Your father is here. Do you want to see him?" she asked.

Luckmane walked over and said something to his father. It was impossible to tell his father's age, but he looked tired. We all did. The earthquake had drained us of energy, chipped away at our hope. The sadness inside didn't shift, but as Luckmane hugged and talked to his siblings, at least I could be happy that he would be reunited with his family.

When he came back to me, Luckmane looked serious.

"You're like a mama to me. I want to stay with you, but…" he paused, looking for the words. "Can you take my sister, Baby, and brother, Ricardo? I want them to come and live with us too."

I had no words. Only tears.

I looked at Pierre-Richard, who smiled back at me with a grin as wide as the National Palace.

"Yes," I said, wiping my face. "I'll take your sister and your brother too."

We talked with Luckmane's father. He told us that he didn't mind. Work was hard to find, and he often had to spend days at a time away from home. He felt badly leaving Baby and Ricardo on their own. "They'll be better with you," he said.

We were getting ready to leave when a woman I'd not met before walked up and said hello. She had a little girl beside her, maybe six or seven years old.

"Will you help me? I've been looking after my niece here since the earthquake, but my husband doesn't want to keep her anymore. He says we've got enough problems of our own. I see you're taking in those three. Will you take Rosekencia too?"

"What about her parents?"

"They were both in prison when it happened."

She didn't need to say any more. Everybody knew that the prison had been almost totally destroyed back in January. There had been rumors of survivors, but nobody had actually seen any.

I looked at the girl. "Rosekencia? That's a pretty name."

She smiled.

"Would you like to come and stay with us? It's only a tent, but you're welcome to join us."

Rosekencia's smile turned brighter. "Yes, Mama, I'd like that."

. . . .

That August night, right before Baby, Rosekencia, and I climbed into our tent and Pierre-Richard, Luckmane, and Ricardo went into theirs, we gave thanks. We sang songs of gratitude into the dark night sky. We shouted of God's faithfulness and cried for His mercy. We clapped and swayed and danced. We hugged and cried some more.

Eight months earlier it had seemed as though the whole country was crushed by the earthquake. Eight hours earlier, I had feared that God was once more about to lead me into the pain of childlessness. But my fears were wrong. God had not abandoned us at all. He was right among us. He was about to resurrect His plans in ways I could never have dreamed.

. . . .

Since moving to Fond Parisien, we had been teaching our children. Each morning we would wash our breakfast things and put the chalkboard and benches in the middle of our patch of land. It was about as simple and basic as you could get, with me the sole teacher and Pierre-Richard helping out. We had no ambition to make it into a bigger school. We just wanted to be obedient to God and hold true to the original vision He had given me through the dreams four years earlier.

In June, as we were saying goodbye to the first children we had taken in, we had a visit from a father with his two teenage boys. Wilner was 17, and Julbert was 15. Their father explained that they lived up in the mountains, a two-hour hike away, but could not afford to go to school there. If he could find a place for his boys to stay near Fond Parisien, he wondered if Pierre-Richard and I would admit them to the school.

We said yes.

Their father put up a basic shelter made out of cardboard and plastic sheeting on a scrap of land nearby at the base of the mountain. He gave his sons responsibility for a herd of goats, and each morning they did their chores around their shelter and then came to school.

They were good kids, always gentle, respectful, and willing to do whatever they were asked. They worked hard with the goats and at school. Though they were far older than the students for whom the curriculum I taught was designed, they had missed so much school over the years that they struggled with some of the work being done by children half their age. It took courage to sit on a school bench next to a child whose raised hand would barely touch their heads. It took so much strength of character to return to the second and third grade and learn the basics all over again. But Wilner and Julbert were some of the bravest people I had ever met.

They needed to be. By the time October came around, other children in the area found out they were sleeping in their simple shelter surrounded by their goats. The kids would visit and shout abuse at them. They'd call them out for being poor and throw rocks at them.

As soon as Wilner told us what was going on, Pierre-Richard and I knew what we needed to say.

"You can stay here, but your father or mother need to come and see us so that we can talk it through properly. If anything happens to you, we will be responsible."

As soon as the words left my mouth, I realized how significant they were.

We were responsible. We weren't just a couple running a budget school under a tent or a shelter for kids that had nowhere else to go. We were responsible in the same way that these children's own birth parents were responsible. And in their absence, we were taking on that parental role.

Wilner and Julbert's father came to see us, and we talked through what it meant for us to become their guardians and how we would have to make decisions about them. We'd had similar conversations with Luckmane, Ricardo, and Baby's father, as well as with Rosekencia's aunt, but somehow with these two boys it felt different. It felt more real because in choosing to live with us, the boys were moving away from their family.

When we had been working in Fonds Baillard, teachers and a church worked with us to feed, teach, and clothe over 100 pupils. Before we started, we had needed plans and systems and strategies in place.

In our little tent school on our tiny scrap of land in Fond Parisien, things were completely different. Nothing about what we were doing felt strategic. We had no game plan, no systems. All we had was a desire to say yes to whatever God invited us to. All we had was a sense in our hearts that we cared for these children as if they were our own.

When they got sick, we hurt with them. When they laughed, we laughed too. And when they called us Mama and Pappy, our eyes teared up and our smiles broke out.

· · · · · · · · · · · · ·

The phone call I received about Rosekencia one night left me shaking with fear. It was her aunt, and she was upset.

"It's Rosekencia's mother," she said between sobs. "She's alive."

For a moment I didn't think anything of it. Since we'd taken Rosekencia in, she had gone through phases of telling us that she was convinced her mom was still alive. She'd bring it up in conversation repeatedly over a few days and then not mention it again for weeks. At first, we did what we could to see if she was right, but every time we searched we found nothing. As far as we could tell, Rosekencia's mother had died when the prison collapsed.

"She's saying that I stole Rosekencia from her," said the aunt. "I don't want to give Rosekencia to her, but she's alive. She's her mother. She should be with her."

Pierre-Richard and I sobbed that night. We knew that if we told the police that Rosekencia's mother had escaped from the prison, they would arrest her again, but we did not want to act out of the flesh. We wanted to act out of love and grace, not fear or hate.

Rosekencia screamed and danced and ran with delight when we told her the next morning. "My mother is alive!" Her words rang out, all the way down to the lake and up to the top of the mountain.

When she calmed a little, she looked at us. "Mama, Pappy, I like being around you, but…"

She didn't need to say anything more. Though our hearts were breaking, hers was healing. How could we keep her from her mother?

. . . .

A week later we said goodbye.

The pain I felt was real and familiar. The same old emptiness deep and cold within me. Years had passed since I grieved this way for the loss of a child, and it hurt just as much as it did when I miscarried, just as much as when I saw the life fade away from Moïka's face.

But pain was not the only thing I felt. I knew I was not alone. Pierre-Richard was beside me, sobbing just as hard. And God was there, too, though not to punish me or to crow over my tears. Finally, I understood that He is not cruel, and He does not delight in our pain. He does not turn His back on us when we hurt. He shares it— every sob, every ache, every breath.

This was the moment I finally broke free from the shame. The weight that had shackled itself to me for years was gone. The pain I felt at saying goodbye to Rosekencia was not a sign of God's judgement, but a sign of His love. I ached because I loved Rose-kencia like she was my own. When I understood that, I understood that God had made good on His promise.

> He gives the barren woman a home, making her the joyous mother of children (Psalm 113:9).

From the moment I'd been given that verse, I always assumed it meant I was going to get pregnant and have children. At first, I thought it would be with Michel, then with Pierre-Richard. Finally, I understood the truth. God was making me a mama in His own unique and perfect way.

11

THE NEW LOWEST POINT

We started the day like any other, listening to the geckos chirping and clicking in the darkness. Pierre-Richard and I watched the children climb out of the tents and smiled as they rubbed their eyes in the predawn darkness. When we were all together, we grabbed our buckets and jerry cans, formed our usual line, and headed off to the spring by the lake a mile down the track. By the time we were ready to turn around and haul our water home, the last traces of sleep had disappeared. The kids started talking excitedly about what lay ahead in school that day.

A typical start to a typical day. As we smeared our peanut butter onto sheets of thin and crumbling yucca bread for breakfast, we talked and laughed and gave thanks to God for all His blessings. We barely noticed the heavy clouds blocking the sunlight throughout the morning or the breeze that brought colder air down from the mountain in the afternoon. We packed up school when it was time to finish, and because it was Friday we said goodbye to the handful of village kids who had started to join us for lessons.

Only one thing was unusual about that day. Rumors about a cholera epidemic in Port-au-Prince had started to reach us in Fond Parisien. We knew it was bad, but midway through the day, Pierre-Richard received a text from a friend. An international media organization had announced that thousands of people had died.

We turned on the radio, but all we got were snatches of static.

I had started boiling water for rice when Pierre-Richard called my name.

"Look at that storm," he said, staring up at the mountain.

It looked as though the sky above the mountain was one giant bruise. But instead of being still or moving slowly, it was alive. Dark blacks and purples and grays swirled together, clouds folding in on themselves, chasing each other in every possible direction. Streaks of rain tied the clouds to the ground. We watched, silent and still, as the storm came down the mountain, heading straight for us.

Before the clouds were above us—before we could do anything at all—a violent wind tore through our tents. The wind brought a wall of rain and hail so harsh it felt like it would rip our skin. Pierre-Richard and I each scooped into our arms as many children as we could and sprinted for the neighbor's house.

The noise of the storm almost drowned out the sound of the children's crying. I paused for a beat and looked out the doorway. Apart from the ground itself, nothing was staying still. The storm was shaking everything, tearing up whatever was in its path.

Pierre-Richard grabbed my hand and pulled me outside. "Come on! We need to save what we can."

I had only been inside a minute, but the storm had grown stronger. The hail was larger and hit harder. It felt like rocks. I crouched and ran to our tents, protecting my face with my arm. Papers filled the air as our benches and cooking pots scraped across the ground.

For a while I was frozen. It couldn't believe that such power and chaos could spring up like that. I stared at the clouds above me, now so dark it felt like night was about to fall.

"Yvrose!"

I turned and saw Pierre-Richard looking at me, his eyes wild with fear. He screamed my name again. "Move!"

I twisted around and saw one of the heavy wooden poles we had used to hold the tarp up. It was as thick as my leg and had come out of the ground. It was flying right at me like a missile.

The sound of the storm fell away, and everything slowed down. I couldn't do anything. I was powerless. There was just me and the wooden post that had me in its sights.

I felt a strong hand on my arm. It was my neighbor, and he pulled me clear of the pole right before it tumbled and crashed on the ground where I had been standing.

"Get inside," Pierre-Richard shouted. "Now!"

I was in no mood to argue, and our neighbor helped me back to his house. I watched as Pierre-Richard struggled for another moment to stop the tarp from getting ripped in half or the tents from being crushed and swept away, but it was no use. Soon he was running back to us as well.

Apart from our children, we had been able to save nothing. All we could do was stand and stare for the next two hours as Hurricane Tomas destroyed what little we had.

    ● ● ● ● ● ● ● ● ● ● ●

I gave up on sleep early the next morning. There were no geckos chirping and no quiet, calm moments in which to anticipate the good things that lay ahead. Only darkness and aching tiredness as we lay crammed on the floor of our neighbor's single room.

When I saw the first traces of light through the open window, I picked my way over the sleeping bodies of my children and opened the door. The wind was gone and the skies clear. It was calm, even peaceful in the air above. I took a deep breath and stepped outside.

For nine months, we had been living on the little patch of land that Pierre-Richard had bought. We hadn't built anything or put up any structures other than a tarp and our two tents, but it was fine for us. We had used scraps of wood, old cinder blocks, and anything else we could find to serve as furniture. We'd designated an area for cooking, another for playing soccer, and another for hanging up laundry. It looked like a refugee camp, but that was okay by us. It was home.

At least, it had been home. In the space of two hours, almost everything had been destroyed by the hurricane. The tarp was ripped to shreds. The wooden stakes that held it had been yanked out of the earth and smashed on the ground. The two tents we slept in were crushed and torn, their frames bent and broken into impossible angles. Our benches and chalkboard—the only pieces of furniture we had that showed we were a functioning school—were either gone or destroyed. The boxes where we kept our books and papers were overturned and empty. The papers themselves were gone, too, with just a handful trapped against the wall at the far end of our land.

Everything in me—all my bones, all my muscles, all my cells—felt heavy. I found a cinder block and lifted it up on its side so I could sit on it. My eyes closed, and waves of tiredness washed over me. But it was not the kind of tiredness that needs a good night of sleep. It was the kind of weary ache you see on the face of the old and the defeated.

I was not yet 50, but I felt old. I had survived the hurricane and avoided cholera, but I was defeated.

I heard a noise and looked up. Pierre-Richard had come outside. He was staring just like I had, trying to take in the full extent of the damage, trying to make sense of it all.

I closed my eyes again. I wanted to concentrate. I wanted to figure out what this all meant.

The words that Moses spoke to his people, the Israelites, came into my mind. "Be strong and courageous. Do not be afraid or terrified because of them, for the Lord your God goes with you; he will never leave you nor forsake you" (Deuteronomy 31:6 NIV).

Then came to mind God's words quoted in Hebrews: "Never will I leave you; never will I forsake you" (Hebrews 13:5 NIV).

Finally, there were the very words of Jesus Himself: "Surely I am with you always, to the very end of the age" (Matthew 28:20 NIV).

I felt the tears flood inside me. Silently, I started to pray.

You'll never leave me. You'll never forsake me. Well, I'm sorry, but I don't believe You.

It felt strange, talking to God like this, but there was nothing I could do to stop the words from shouting out within me.

You have not kept Your promise. You have not kept Your word. You told me to come and live by faith, and so here I am sleeping under a tent. People must think I'm crazy to be here and live like this, but I did it because You told me to.

But now there's this. Don't You see it? Don't You care? Everything we've built here is ruined. How could You let this happen?

It makes no sense.

The words stopped as soon as they had started. I felt bad for saying them, bad for talking to God this way, but I could not ask for forgiveness. I was too empty inside.

So I sat on my cinder block, in silence, and waited.

I waited while the children got up and walked around. I waited while Pierre-Richard fixed them some breakfast. I waited while he started repairing one of the tents, and the kids either helped him or tidied other places.

The sun was fully up when I saw Pierre-Richard had stopped

working on the tent. He was staring at me, holding something in front of his face.

A camera?

"What are you doing?" I shouted, hot tears on my cheeks, a searing pain in my heart. "How can you even think of taking a photograph at a time like this? Can't you see what's happening? Everything's ruined. Everything's over."

I couldn't stop the sobbing after that. Not even when some of the kids came over and cuddled up beside me. Not even when Pierre-Richard came over and held me. Not even when he bent his head close to mine and whispered, "God has not abandoned us, Yvrose. He is about to rescue us. That's why I took the photo, because this is a moment one day you and I will want to celebrate."

* * * * * * * * * * * *

For the rest of the morning, Pierre-Richard and the children worked hard to clear our property. I did what I could, but the heaviness was so great that I wasn't much help. I would spend a few minutes picking up papers or searching for kitchen utensils that had been scattered, but then I'd feel sad and empty again, needing to sit down.

A house was being built nearby. It had two rooms, and the building had stopped before they managed to fit any doors. The owner was going to rent it out if he got around to finishing it. All day I found my eyes drawn to it. Each time I stopped and stared, I felt worse about our situation. I could taste the bitterness inside my mouth.

If God really had our back, we wouldn't be living in a tent.

When we first moved to Fond Parisien, I had looked at our little scrap of land with love. There were houses nearby, and every one of our neighbors lived in better conditions than we did. I didn't care.

Our land was small, covered in rocks, and didn't even have a single tree to provide shade, but it was home. It was the place where God had led us—the place where I knew that I had finally become Mama.

Not anymore.

The rocky emptiness taunted me. What kind of idiot was I for thinking that anything good could grow on soil like this? Our home had been wiped out, our hope destroyed. Even if we could manage to clear it up and fix everything that the hurricane had broken, the damage was too much. I'd lost confidence that God could sustain us here.

I'd never felt this low before, and it frightened me.

It wasn't like the night when I was in the hospital in Spain and told God to leave me. That was a moment when I turned my back on God. It was my choice, my mistake, my selfishness.

This was different. I felt like God had turned His back on me. And that was the most terrifying prospect of all.

*   *   *   *   *   *   *   *   *   *   *   *

My phone rang in the afternoon.

"Yvrose? It's Susan." It took me a moment to place her. Susan and I worked together for a while when I lived in Fairhaven, Massachusetts. She was a nursing assistant like me. We weren't what I'd call friends. I didn't even know she had my number.

"Hey," I said.

"I saw the news about the hurricane, and I've been thinking about you. Are you okay?"

How could I even begin to answer that? Part of me wanted to tell her that I was feeling as though my life had pretty much been destroyed and that God had abandoned me, but I couldn't find the words. "Fine, I guess."

"Yvrose, I can't get you out of my mind. Every time I think about you, I pray. And every time I pray, I keep on thinking that I need to talk to you. I need to do something, but I don't know what. So I got your number. I guess what I'm calling for is to say that I want to know how I can help you."

It was kind of her to say, but I was tired and not in the mood for much more talking. "Thanks, Susan. Prayer is always good."

"No, Yvrose." Something had changed in her voice. She was speaking with authority now. "I want to know—what do you need right now? I want to know so that I can help you."

I let out the longest breath.

And as I inhaled, I felt the truth light up within me. The tears came quickly, too, and for quite some time I could not speak.

"Yvrose? Yvrose?" Susan's voice brought me back.

I sniffed and wiped my face. My voice sounded fragile and new.

"Susan, you don't know what this means. Two hours ago, I was sitting here telling God that He had forsaken me. I need to repent for saying that. I was wrong. He has not left me. I know that because He put me in your mind and led you to call. Thank you."

"I'm so glad." I could hear Susan's smile in her voice. "But you still haven't told me what you need. I want to know."

I knew exactly what I wanted, but it still felt like a risk to ask. What if I told her and she said no? What would that mean about God? Could I really ask for so much from someone I hardly knew?

"Yvrose, come on. Tell me."

"Okay," I said, my voice trembling. "We're all living in tents and I don't want to do it anymore. There's a little house across the street and I want to move there, but I can't afford it. That's what I want."

"Thank you," said Susan. "I'm going to send you the rent."

• • • • • • • • • • • •

When God moves, He really moves. Soon after I finished the call with Susan and told Pierre-Richard about her offer, the owner of the house came by to check on his property after the storm. Pierre-Richard and I asked if we could rent it as it was. He looked at us like we were crazy, then he saw the flattened tents and torn tarp behind us. We did the deal right then and there.

That night, before we ate the last of the rice that we had been able to save, we stood in the house and sang the loudest praises we'd ever sang to God. We clapped until our hands felt sore and sang until our voices cracked.

"God has done something great today," I said to the children as we stood in a circle. "He has allowed us to feel desperate. He has let us come down into the pit so that we might know how mighty and loving He is as He rescues us. Because we have experienced this fear, we know that He comforts us. Because we have felt such sorrow, we can now feel His joy."

· · · · · · · · · · · ·

The hurricane was the beginning of something precious and profound in our lives. It was the start of a new understanding of what Jesus meant when He said, "Do not worry." It was not the end of poverty or the last moment we experienced danger, risk, or need. There have been so many of those times since then. What has changed is the way we approach them. Instead of feeling a great need and worrying it means God has abandoned us, we have learned to look for God's rescue, to trust His love, and rejoice in the opportunity He gives us to remember that He alone sustains us.

God will use anything and anyone to bring about His plans and His purposes.

12

THE HEALING HAS BEGUN

I could tell that Pierre-Richard was feeling the same surge of emotions as me the day we met Esther. We were both holding back the tears from the moment we first saw her lifted carefully out of the car. She wasn't even three years old, but her body was covered in burns.

Esther stood beside her godmother and stared, sizing us up. It was obvious that every part of her was focused on one single question: Will I be safe here?

Every part of me wanted to reach out and hug her. I wanted to tell her that she would be safe with us and that our hearts were open to her, but I knew I needed to hold back. Esther needed time to stare and think. While she did, her godmother talked.

"Her mother died a year ago. She left Esther and two boys, one older, one younger. Nobody knew where the father was, so they were sent to live with their grandmother in the city. She loved Esther and paid her more attention than she paid the brothers. The little one grew jealous. Last month he pushed her into the fire. I took her in and looked after her."

The godmother paused. Saying what came next caused her pain. "I can't keep her."

It was an unusual thing for a godmother to say. Becoming a godparent in Haiti is a serious responsibility. We accept the duty on the understanding that we will be the one to take a child in as our own if their birth parent dies. "You look healthy," I said to Esther's godmother. "Why can't you take her?"

"I'm a nursing student, and the school provides accommodation for me, but they won't let me keep her."

It made sense, but even though I could feel the love for Esther grow within me, this was a big decision. We needed to take time.

After a week of praying and making sure that Esther's story really was as her godmother said—including seeing a copy of her mother's death certificate—Esther and her godmother traveled to Fond Parisien again. This time, Esther stayed.

Esther's godmother would visit from time to time. Whenever Esther saw her, she would hide. It could take much time for us to find her, and then all our effort to persuade her to come out and say hello. Finally, after the third or fourth visit like this, I had a hunch about what was bothering her.

I left Pierre-Richard talking with Esther's godmother and crawled into the corner of the tent where she was hiding. Two big eyes peered out from behind a blanket.

"We're not sending you away," I said. "You're with us forever."

From that day on, Esther relaxed. Knowing that she belongs here has changed things for her. She's become a key part of our family, and our family has grown stronger because of her. She is different from all the other girls. She's not sassy or extroverted. She observes the world from a safe place—usually at my side. She's organized, careful, and caring. Even though she's one of the youngest of the family, she's like a mother to many.

· · · · · · · · · · · ·

Even before Esther joined us, our family had been growing quickly. By the time the first anniversary of the earthquake came around in January 2011, we had Luckmane, Baby, Ricardo, Rosekencia, Wilner, and Julbert. We had also been joined by Nacius, who wore the biggest smile I had ever seen on a boy, and his sister Sonita, who rarely spoke and wouldn't look any of us in the eyes. We did not have long to wait until more children came. First we welcomed two more boys, Maiky and Merson, then two more girls, Myrlande and Judelle.

Twelve children. My heart had never felt so full. We were living in our two-room home, fetching water together each morning and cooking before setting up for school under what we'd rescued of the tarp. Life was full. And it was about to get even more so.

One of my brothers, Jean Claude, married an older woman. She had children of her own from a previous marriage, and they were all grown up. Despite the fact that she told him she didn't want to get pregnant, she conceived.

My brother came up with a solution. He asked whether Pierre-Richard and I would be willing to take the child. This time there was no need to do background research like we did with Esther. We simply rejoiced, gave thanks to God, and told Jean Claude we would be happy to adopt the child as our own.

Saying goodbye to a child is never easy. The day that Pierre-Richard and I traveled to Leogane in the south of Haiti to my brother's house, it wasn't just the tiny baby in his wife's arms who was crying. Though it was hard, it was also right.

Pierre-Richard and I drove back home, beaming. We were proud parents of a baby boy, and we couldn't wait to introduce him to his brothers and sisters waiting at home. We talked about names. Pierre-Richard had some ideas, but nothing concrete. I told him that I had only one idea, but I knew it was a good one.

"What is it? Tell me!"

"Pierre-Richardson."

Pierre-Richardson was our thirteenth child, and he brought a new level of love and joy into our home. His 12 siblings loved on him from the moment they first met, and each morning when we prepared for school, they would take turns arranging his toys in the little space they created for him at the side of our classroom area. Seeing them open their hearts to him like this made Pierre-Richard and me happy in ways we'd never imagined.

．．．．．．．．．．．．．

When Wilner and Julbert came to live with us, I thought no other children could ever be so polite and considerate. I told people then what I tell them now—that when God gives, He gives good things. I believe today just as I believed back then that He hand-picked our children, bringing us the right ones at the right times.

In the early days, we needed the calmness of Wilner and the easy smiles and hugs from Luckmane. Rosekencia's sass made us smile, and we were ready for Nacius's energy. The larger our family became, the more confident Pierre-Richard and I grew as parents. God never tested us beyond what—with His help—we could handle. Having a baby living with us in the tents brought its own challenges, but our joy at having him made it all worthwhile. He gave this barren woman a home and made her the joyous mother of all the children in her care. And we were joined by more children—Lovens, Ifnold, and Vance—next also welcoming Celicia, Wilner and Julbert's older sister, who came to help me with the cooking and caring for Richardson and Vance. We were a family of 19 living in a space smaller than most American garages.

We couldn't have been happier.

. . . .

When Judelle arrived, we knew that God was inviting us to say yes to Him, even though it was the greatest challenge we had yet faced. She was from Port-au-Prince, and her mother was a prostitute. Judelle had lived with her under a tarp near my sister until her uncle became concerned and took her to live with him. When the earthquake destroyed his home, Judelle went back to living under a tarp. Her neighborhood was one of the worst in the city, and the uncle knew that if Judelle did not get out soon, her life would take some dangerous and dark paths.

My sister, Idoxie, told Judelle's family that Pierre-Richard and I might be able to help. She arranged a meeting for us all, and we agreed to go home and pray. As with all our children, we needed to be sure that we were the right home for them, and that the story we were being told about Judelle was true. Sadly, too many children in Haiti are abandoned, mistreated, or trafficked each year, and many lies are told to cover up the truth. We have always been careful to make sure that we have not been deceived and that we know the truth about the children we welcome into the family.

Everything about Judelle was as we had been told. Even her behavior backed up the story about her troubled early life. Due to her past sexual abuse, she played in ways that no four-year-old should learn to play.

At first, we feared that it was too much for us to handle. We felt instantly protective of the other children and deeply heartbroken for Judelle. We wanted to change the script right away, to instantly reset Judelle to the kind of innocent, free child that we knew she was supposed to be. But we were painfully aware of the fact that there were no quick fixes—no switch to be flicked. We guessed that whatever change was going to happen within her was going to take years.

We didn't factor in God, though.

We prayed for Judelle so much. We'd wake up in the morning before sunrise and call on God to come down and heal her. We stayed up late into the night, begging God not to forget this little girl, pleading with Him to show mercy.

God did not turn His back on us. Slowly at first, but with a gathering force that soon became unmistakable, Judelle changed. She stopped using the language she had used when she first came to us. She changed the way she played with the toys we had around the yard. She interacted with the other kids in a whole bunch of ways. She even started to look different.

Within just three months, she was a new child altogether. She had forgotten all about the darkness of her past. She was restored.

As we approached the one-year anniversary of her coming to live with us, we received a phone call. It was from her mother.

"You've got my daughter, Judelle. My brother is coming to get her."

One thing that hadn't changed throughout the year was the way Judelle talked about her uncle. She loved him deeply, and everything we knew about him told us he was a good man. Judelle's mom explained that her brother was no longer homeless and he was able once again to take his niece in and look after her.

Again, we needed to make sure the story was all she said. When we were sure that we had been told the truth, we took Judelle back.

As we drove west, I could not stop my mind from returning to the day we took Luckmane back to Port-au-Prince. I had been sure I was going to return home childless that day, but instead we had a backseat full of children. I wondered whether the same thing was going to happen again with Judelle.

It didn't. We said goodbye and felt every stab of pain as we watched her leave, hand in hand with her uncle.

But God did not challenge us beyond what we could cope with. God sustained us. He was as present in our sorrow at saying goodbye as He had been in our joy at seeing the innocent, trusting, God-designed Judelle emerge.

* * * * * * * * * * * *

Seeing Judelle transform so quickly unlocked something in me, too—courage. Specifically, the courage to ask the one question that had plagued me all my life. I wanted to know if I would ever give birth to my own child.

Ever since the death of Moïka and the following abortions, this had been the one question I avoided. I had been too scared of the answer being "no," because if it was, then my fear that I was being punished by God for my sin would be right. So I had taken matters into my own hands. I had become promiscuous at first, and then, with Michel, I had lost faith. I had walled off that part of my heart, only allowing God in when I was broken and grieving after yet another miscarriage.

It was different now. On most days I could look around me and see a tent full of evidence that God had already made me a mama. I could easily remind myself that He had not forgotten me, and I knew He had given me children. On good days, I could drink deeply and feel satisfied whenever the kids called me Mama.

Not every day was a good day. Sometimes I would hear a whisper of doubt within me. Was I really a mother to these children? They could be taken away at any time. Did I really hold them the way a birth mother held them?

I did not like these thoughts and wanted them to stop. So I reminded myself that God's love was a reality in my life, and when

I started to pray, I did so not from a place of fear or shame. I asked like any child would ask a loving, wise, caring parent.

"Father God," I prayed. "Are You ever going to give me any children of my own?"

I decided to let these words echo for a few days. I trusted God and knew that He would reveal what He wanted to reveal in good time. There was no need for me to pester Him.

But a couple of days later, I gave up on being patient. It was time to pester.

"God, You promised me kids and I want one that comes out of my belly. I'm surrounded by wonderful children that I love more deeply than I ever thought I could. But please, I just need to know: Are these the kids You promised me, or do I need to persist and keep on trying to get pregnant with Pierre-Richard?"

I did not hear a booming voice or see a blinding light, but I knew He was speaking to me. And God's answer was clear, and it was perfect.

"These are the kids. They don't grow out of your stomach. They grow out of your heart. And that's the best place to have somebody grow. If you care for them, you will find joy."

. . . .

Years later I was reading my Bible when I found a passage that reminded me of the day God told me there would be no children for me to grow in my belly. It was the part in Genesis 18 where God wonders out loud about hiding from Abraham what He plans to do to Sodom and Gomorrah. A simple truth struck me—God shares His plans with His friends. He did it with Abraham that day, and He did it with David and so many others. If He was revealing things to me, then I must have been in the right place.

That's why it was so significant to know that the children we had taken in were the ones God had planned for us. It didn't just allow me to stop worrying about getting pregnant. It revealed that Pierre-Richard and I were right where God wanted us to be. It reminded us that we were not alone, but with Him.

When you're in that place, freedom abounds—freedom to act boldly, freedom to ignore fear, and freedom for me to be Mama and Pierre-Richard to be Pappy and for the two of us to fight to protect our own children with our lives.

We needed every last ounce of that freedom when things started to go wrong at home.

Unlike Luckmane and Baby, Ricardo had dropped out of school, though most people his age had long since completed their schooling. He was not interested in learning, and the years he had spent in Port-au-Prince had left their mark on him. His father would go missing for days at a time, and Ricardo had gotten involved in things he was too young for. He had grown up far too fast.

When Ricardo had been with us for two years, he called one of the girls into a room and told her to have sex with him. She ran straight out and told us. Ricardo admitted it, and the decision was made. I called his father and told him to come and get him.

Knowing we were caring for the very children whom God had picked out for us made it a simple decision. Not easy, perhaps, but simple. These children were ours. We would defend them with everything we had, from any threat they faced—even if that threat came from within.

* * * * * * * * * * * *

If the earthquake taught me anything, it was that I am utterly powerless to save my own life. I am trained as a nurse and an educator, and I know the theory of fixing bodies and nurturing young minds. I believe in the application of science and the value of

learning. But powerful as these things are, they are nothing compared to the power of God. That goes for healing too. Only God can
truly heal and transform our lives. Only God can bring the change
that Ricardo, Judelle's mom, and Esther's little brother need. Only
God.

Sometimes I wish I had learned to trust God earlier in my life.
How much pain would I have saved myself if I had learned to lean
wholly on Him when my life first started to break up? How much
heartache would I have avoided?

Painful as parts of my life have been, I am grateful for the way
God has met me in the midst of my darkest moments. I am grateful
for the fact that I know for myself how fully God can transform a
life. And I am grateful for the fact that I can never doubt His power
to heal. For of all the healing and restoration I have seen in lives like
Judelle's and Esther's, Julbert's and Luckmane's, the greatest healing
of all has been in my own.

God saw me in my broken, wounded, barren state and sat with
me. He did not tell me to leave my pain behind before He would
accept me. He sat with me. He wept with me. He held me. And
gradually, when the time was right, He finally let me see the truth
of my life. He showed me that through all the years when I wanted
a child, I was not ready to have one. I truly believe the child would
have been an idol to me. I would have put all my hope in his or her
love, not in God. And if anything had happened to that child, all the
pain and guilt and fear would have raged to the surface once again—
more fiercely than ever.

I don't believe that God broke me. I don't believe that He caused
my miscarriages. I believe He redeemed them. And I know that
when I finally was ready, His healing touch was enough to change
everything.

13

THE RICHES OF
BEING POOR

Our little school in Fond Parisien grew quickly. One year after the earthquake, we had 28 children on our roll. A year later that number had risen to 100. And though my 401(k) had long since been drained, and Pierre-Richard's account was empty, somehow we were able to afford to employ a couple of extra teachers to join me. We gathered every day underneath the tarp—a new one that the UN gave us not long after the hurricane—and went through a simple curriculum I had used at the school in Fonds Baillard.

Although the school was growing and our family was expanding as well, some things didn't change. Each morning, while the skies were still dark, we lined up and walked the mile down to the lake to fetch water. We weren't the only ones there, and the spring was covered in trash. We taught the kids how to use a bowl to scoop the water into the buckets and how to filter out the trash, though a lot of them were better at it than Pierre-Richard and I were.

At the end of the day, we'd all repeat the journey, washing ourselves down in the lake first before filtering out the trash and refilling the buckets with the water we'd need for cooking that night's meal. It had been years since I carried a bucket on my head, but with a little practice, the skill came back.

The children never complained about living this way. Pierre-Richard, on the other hand, would definitely get a little cranky if we didn't have any food to eat. Whenever that happened, he'd take a tap-tap and go in search of money. Sometimes he'd go see his mom in Port-au-Prince and ask her; other times he'd track down someone who owed him money from when he used to trade in cell phones before we met. The smile on his face whenever he came back with a one-pound bag of flour or rice was always infectious. While I made dumplings, some of the kids would go off in search of any scraps of timber they could find to use as firewood because we couldn't afford charcoal. Others would look for moringa trees and come home with a few fistfuls of leaves. I'd cook them up with flour and plantains as a *bouillon*, a Haitian stew. We'd share our bowls and thank God for feeding us yet again.

As parents, Pierre-Richard and I were desperate to make sure that our kids grew up with praise on their lips. Not long after we moved to Fond Parisien, we made the decision to start and end every day with prayer and worship.

I got the idea from Telfort. He was living over the border in the Dominican Republic, and I took a couple of days to visit him, his wife, Getrude, and their six children. I arrived late at night and woke up the next morning to a sound I could not discern. At first, I thought it was an army of geckos all chirping in time, but then I realized it was clapping—rhythmic, steady, and full of life—with voices singing over it. I followed the music and found Gertude, Tel-fort, and their girls standing in a circle outside. Eyes closed, hearts open, they sang songs of love and thanks to God. I could feel my breath grow heavy within me, and the presence of God was thick. I closed my eyes and sank into it, joining in the simple songs that spoke of God's never-ending, unbreakable love for us.

Gertrude guided us, and as one song ended, the rhythms we made with our hands would change subtly, folding into another song. When we had sung our last, Gertrude called out Scripture references, and we recited the verses. She talked about God's faithfulness and His love and how the day ahead would present so many opportunities for each of us to know, to serve, and to follow God more closely. We prayed, then hugged, and when it ended, I stood there, feeling a little stunned.

It lasted for almost an hour, but it felt like minutes. And for the rest of the day, God felt close in ways I had not experienced since my first days with Marie. To my joy, we repeated the clapping, praising, and praying at night. I went to sleep with my hands warm from clapping and my heart full from knowing God's love.

I came back to Haiti and decided to do the same, giving the first and the last of our focus every day to God.

Between the busyness of a large and growing family and the busyness of a large and growing school, I barely thought about my own standard of living. It didn't occur to me that it was an odd thing for a woman who owned an American passport to be carrying water in a bucket on her head. The way I saw it, we couldn't afford to buy drinking water, and the spring was the nearest water source to our home. Therefore, God had provided, and I was grateful. After the earthquake and the hurricane, I had stopped trying to make my own plans and pin them on God. I was just trying to trust Him completely. If that meant I needed to fetch my own water or flavor our stews using leaves from nearby trees, then that was fine by me. Never once did we run out of things to thank God for at the start and end of the day. His kindness never failed us.

I didn't think of myself as poor. At least, not until I had a visit from an old friend.

Rosemary and I had attended the same church in Charlotte. We kept in contact when I moved to Haiti, and she was one of a number of friends who prayed faithfully for me. When she found out that she was coming to Haiti for a conference where she was going to train churches, schools, and leaders how to deal with trauma, she made sure she extended her trip so that she could come visit us at the end.

Pierre-Richard went to get her on a Sunday morning. We had finished our regular church service in the yard, and I had just said goodbye to the neighbors who had started coming. I looked up to see Rosemary standing on the track that ran alongside our yard. She was looking around and hadn't noticed me staring at her. I called out her name, and a broad smile immediately snapped back onto her face.

She screamed with delight and ran over. We hugged for the longest time. "Yvrose! It's so good to see you. Look at you!"

It felt so good to see Rosemary again, and I quickly called the kids over and introduced them one by one. Some of the younger ones looked a little wide-eyed, and it took me a moment to figure out that Rosemary was probably the first white person that Pierre-Richardson and Judelle had ever hugged.

We sat on benches and talked for an hour, barely pausing for breath. Rosemary told me about life in Charlotte, and I shared about life in Haiti. We both had so much to thank God for.

I showed her around the school and our home. She didn't say much as she stepped inside the house. I was going to ask whether she was hungry when someone called me outside.

"Mama?" It was one of the neighboring kids who had been with us at church. He held out a fish to me. "My father saw you had a visitor, so he sent this for you."

I thanked him and his father for being so kind, and my sister Idoxie, who was visiting, prepared a fire on which to cook it. Rosemary sat next to me in silence and watched the kids play soccer. The ball had long ago been punctured, but they still chased around after it, screaming with delight.

When the fish was fried, Idoxie put it on a plate and offered it to Rosemary.

She swallowed hard and looked away.

"What is it, Rosemary?"

"Oh, Yvrose. I can't eat that fish."

I was confused. Had I forgotten about some dietary restrictions? "I'm sorry," I said, "but this is all we have. Can't you eat fish?"

Rosemary laughed. "No, it's not that. It's...I mean, how can I eat it when you all look so hungry? What will you all eat?"

I could feel my chest beginning to grow tight, but I smiled and shook my head. "It's fine, Rosemary. This is our gift to you. Please, take it."

Rosemary started crying. "Yvrose, are you happy?"

It was my turn to cry, though I didn't know why. I was happy. I really was. "Yes," I said, forcing a deep breath in. "I am."

"Then I'm happy for you. But you know you're always welcome to come back. You don't have to live like this."

I thought back to the time when we both lived in Charlotte. Rosemary had seen me living a normal American life. I was a teacher who, with bonuses, could earn $70,000 a year. I had credit cards and car payments. I loved shoes, but only if they were real leather and had heels. I had no time for flats. I liked jewels, too, especially gold and diamonds. Perfume was another luxury that I allowed myself, as well as eating out at good seafood restaurants. And if I could take any of my nieces or nephews to Disney World, I was that auntie who returned them to their parents with bags full of gifts and eye-popping amounts of candy.

I remembered it like it was someone else's life.

"I know I could go back to America, Rosemary. Maybe I could even go back to life as it was. But what I know for sure is that there's nowhere else I want to be than here right now. God asked me to live by faith, and that's what I'm doing."

• • • • • • • • • • • •

The conversation with Rosemary was like a pair of new glasses. From the moment we sat on either side of that plate of uneaten fish, my life did not look the same to me. I saw it more clearly. For the first time since moving to Haiti, I finally understood that I really was living in poverty.

In the days that followed, I started looking at other people in Fond Parisien. It's not a wealthy town at all, but I struggled to find anyone who appeared to be living on less than we were. Everyone could afford to cook on charcoal. Nobody had to buy rice or flour in such small quantities as we did. And it struck me that we never had to wait in line when we collected water down by the lake. Nobody slept in tents like we had, and I couldn't see another house that was lacking doors or shutters for the windows like ours.

Yet here we were, living in one of the poorest countries in the world, and we were considered poor. In our little town, we were the lowest of the low. We were the ones that people pitied.

It was a shock to see all this. But it did not shake my faith.

Ever since the hurricane, Pierre-Richard and I had known that God was able to care for our every need. He had been teaching us to rely on Him for everything, and barely a day went by when we didn't have an opportunity to thank God for stepping in and proving Himself to be faithful once again.

Often, He brought people to us. Like our neighbor offering the fish to feed Rosemary, we were constantly meeting people who were generous and kind. Sometimes they were friends or neighbors; at other times they were strangers.

One day, a couple turned up at the house. I could tell from their accents that they were not from Port-au-Prince, but from the north—a mountainous area where I had not spent much time.

"We brought you this," they said, holding out a papaya. "God told us to bring it to you a month ago, but we couldn't make it here until today."

The timing was perfect. We'd not eaten at all that day.

God continued to amaze us with the way that He called all kinds of different people to help. The UN visited one day, bringing a quarter of a cow and boxes of food. There were vegetables, oranges, and bananas, plus so much milk. It was enough to last our family two weeks, but without even a cooler—let alone a refrigerator—we ate what we could and shared the rest with our school and neighbors.

A group of Muslims brought us rice, beans, and milk powder, and even a young voodoo priest made a visit and told us that he didn't know why, but he felt that he needed to give us a gift of beans. We said thank you and asked if he wanted to receive the gift of salvation in Jesus Christ. He laughed and said, "Some other time."

"I'll hold you to that!" I called out as he smiled and walked away. "The love of God is chasing after you!"

At first I found it humbling to see myself the way Rosemary did. I used to be the person who sent money back to Haiti, a woman who never needed to ask anyone for anything. But now I was poor. Now I was the one waiting for people to come and help me.

All those people who came—the neighbors, the people from

afar, the Muslims, the UN, the voodoo priest—proved to me how dependable God is. They showed me that help will always come because God's love for His children is so great. He always provides. He never lets go.

Living with empty stores and our eyes open to God made an impact on our family. Pierre-Richard and I understood we had to be clear with the children about exactly what was going on, that it was a wonderful gift to them to grow up knowing every single thing we need can be found in God. In choosing to share the burdens of our prayers, we also got to share the joy of our thanks when God responded.

When I first came to Haiti, I was tempted to think I deserved a better standard of living than the people I was serving. That's why I didn't live in Fonds Baillard but rented a room in the house with a doctor and a businesswoman in Fond Parisien. I was proud of the fact that I had returned to Haiti from one of the wealthiest countries in the world, a place where so many people want to live. I saw myself as different from the villagers. It's shameful to admit, but I actually believed I had made a real sacrifice to leave the U.S. and move to Haiti. I was doing something great—or so I thought. How many other people turned their backs on a life of luxury and chose to live among the poor?

Arrogance can suffocate so much of what God would do through us. Being separate from people only served to block up the good work that God had planned for me. I never want people to think that I see myself as separate from others. All I ever want is for people to see God in me. I want to be humble, not put myself above others. I want to be human, honest, weak, and show that all my hope is in God alone.

All this has brought me to one simple but powerful conclusion: If there's a choice between poverty and wealth, I'd rather be poor.

I've known the wealth of a healthy bank balance and a credit card

I can use without having to think twice. I know my way around a good menu as well as an upscale shopping mall. There's really nothing wrong with being wealthy. It's at God's discretion that some are given financial riches. It's what we do with those resources that counts. And for me, wealth didn't lead to much. I was able to help people in Haiti, and I enjoyed being generous with my nieces and nephews, but the good feelings those things gave me never sank deeply or lasted too long. The hole never got filled.

But poverty? That's a different story.

Is it good to be poor? I don't know. But I know that out of my nothing I have found a level of joy and peace I never came close to before. And I know that when you're economically poor, it's so much easier to be spiritually rich.

When you spend your days dependent on God, when your very belly reminds you how much you need Him, there's a depth to the experience that is impossible to ignore. When you spend your hours in eager anticipation, wondering just what wild and crazy way God is going to show His love and care for you next, it's impossible not to feel your faith grow within you.

Material wealth is nothing without someone to parade it in front of. We need those compliments about our house or our car or whatever to make us feel as though our status has been improved. But spiritual wealth is different. Being spiritually rich doesn't require an audience. It's just a matter for us and God. When we're rich in Him, we stop having to strive so hard to impress people.

So I'd rather be poor in things but rich inside in ways that nobody sees. I don't care if nobody knows.

All I care about is that I stay close to God. And trust me, if that's what you want, too, there's nothing like poverty for bringing you to a place where you really have to depend upon Him.

PART FOUR

14

ALL THINGS NEW

Fond Parisien, Haiti. December 30, 2010.

The moment Bill Montgomery pulled up next to our compound, killed his truck's engine, and stood, smiling and waving his Indiana Jones hat in greeting, I had a hunch that God was up to something. Some of the kids, however, weren't so sure. They'd met a few Americans before, but never a white-haired, white-bearded farmer from Missouri who looked like an Old Testament prophet mixed with Santa Claus.

When you're learning to live by faith, you get used to God advancing His plans in unusual ways through unusual people. You learn to listen to God's Spirit, to make judgments not so much on appearance but on the still, small voice that speaks to you. Bill's voice was soft and gentle, but the way that God spoke through him was as loud and large as the hurricane that had torn through the compound earlier in 2010.

After Bill introduced himself, he explained that he was constructing metal homes for orphanages and the elderly. His eyes took in the compound. "Lady, I heard you are a U.S. citizen. What are you doing here?"

"God sent me here."

"Are you sure?"

"Yes."

I told him about the dreams I'd had back in Charlotte, how I'd left the U.S. to start the work here. I told him a little about the first school in Fonds Baillard and the earthquake and the hurricane. I talked about the way the school was growing (now well over 150 pupils) and introduced him to all the children living with us. I told him that we were trying to be obedient to God by loving and serving these kids whom He had brought across our paths. All told, I was talking for quite a while.

Bill had been listening quietly, playing with his hat, staring at it with a furrowed brow. I didn't feel judged or as though Bill was trying to figure me out. I just felt like somehow God was at work.

"Well," Bill said eventually, "in that case I have something for you. We will bring you two houses. All you have to do is clear the land and tell me where you want me to put them."

. . . .

Bill made good on his word and returned the next week to build the foundations for two metal houses. He visited us regularly, bringing food and water in his truck and saving us hours of fetching it from the lake. He gave us money and even a car. Every visit was a gift from God, fueling our songs of thanks and worship that filled the skies twice each day.

God didn't just stop at Bill's gifts. He introduced us to a community in the mountains where we later set up a school for adults. Bill also brought others into our lives, including Pastor Rod Baker—a man with a voice of thunder who encouraged and supported us in so many ways, like building the metal houses on the foundations Bill Montgomery had laid.

Gradually, more people came from all over the world. The UN had a base in Fond Parisien, and through it we were introduced to a nonprofit from Spain that started delivering us food and water. We began to receive help from an Irish nonprofit called Haven, and when a British missionary living in the U.S. visited, she introduced her daughter-in-law, and we started receiving support from a little village called Bolney in southern England.

None of these relationships were planned, and none of them were the result of Pierre-Richard and me trying to think strategically about how to grow a support base. We were simply being open to God, trusting Him, relying on Him, saying "yes" to Him whenever He showed up by bringing another seemingly random person into our lives.

We weren't surprised. Pierre-Richard and I wanted to depend on God, but not only for His resources—we wanted to have Him set our vision and goals as well. Ever since the earthquake, we had been asking God to enlarge our territory and bless the work of our hands (1 Chronicles 4:9-10). Seeing people come from all over the world to lend their help was another unexpected demonstration of the way God works.

* * * * * * * * * * * * *

We needed extra support badly. Our little family wasn't so little anymore—Pierre-Richard and I were now Mama and Pappy to 17 beautiful children. And in the same way that we were learning how to rely on God to meet our needs for food and shelter, He was also teaching us to rely on Him as parents. Central to this new reliance was prayer.

One morning before church, Pastor Jean warned me that I was going to receive a phone call from a man who ran an orphanage and needed help. I felt myself stiffen up a little, but not because I was about to be asked to help. I've just never liked the word *orphanage*. To me, it's always felt cold, impersonal, and the opposite of everything Pierre-Richard and I felt called to do here in Fond Parisien. As far as I know, there's only one word that fits what we're doing here: *family*. We're not an institution or a facility. We're a bunch of people whose lives God has woven together by love.

All that day I waited for the man to phone, but he didn't. He didn't phone the next day either. Days passed, and I put it out of my mind.

The call came at midnight almost a week after Pastor Jean had spoken to me. The man on the other end of the line was anxious and talking so frantically that it took me a while to fully understand what he was saying. He told me about a pastor who had taken in some orphans. He'd provided them with a house to stay in, but for some reason he had now changed his mind.

The man on the phone was panicking. "I tried asking him to let them stay, but he refuses. Says he's had enough of their behavior, that it has always been his plan to live here and he never meant the kids to stay here so long. He's kicking the children out."

"When?"

"Tonight."

I told him that Pierre-Richard and I needed a few moments to talk. The whole situation was wild, and there were many unanswered questions about the children themselves. We didn't know their ages, backgrounds, or even their names. But we knew they were in trouble and needed help. We prayed quickly, and both had the sense that this was a situation where we needed to help out.

"Okay," I said when I called him back. "We'll send someone to get them now, and they can come stay here with us for a few days. We need to meet them and then see if we can help more."

A friend in the city collected them and took them to her home for the night. Pierre-Richard and I traveled in the next morning, and we were instantly surprised. It turned out that the five "kids" weren't little kids after all. Micah, the oldest, was 22 years old, while Fabienne was the youngest and had just turned 16. There were three more young men: Fito and Julmis were both 20, and Julmis's little brother, Stenio, was 16 and didn't talk at all. But Pierre-Richard and I both still had the same sense that God wanted us to help, so we took them with us to Fond Parisien.

Within a few days, we discovered that they weren't just naughty: They were feral.

Each of them had been living on the streets until they were 11 years old. They'd survived by begging and doing who knows what else. And while the man who had asked us to take them was clearly a good and kind Christian, he had not been able to provide them with the kind of structure they needed. They'd gone to church while living in the pastor's house, but none of them lived like they were trusting Jesus and trying to follow His lead. At times, I wondered if the orphanage felt more like a frat house. Maybe the pastor had some good reasons for wanting to be able to move them off his property.

Thanks to Bill's support, we no longer had to march down to the lake every day, but there were still plenty of chores to do each day. We shared them equally among all our children, and even though Micah, Stenio, Julmis, Fito, and Fabienne were staying with us temporarily, we gave them the same duties as everyone else. Unsurprisingly, all five of them found it hard to adjust to these new expectations and responsibilities. But it was the oldest of the five, Micah, who found it hardest. He wanted to remind us of the fact that he was independent, older. It felt inevitable that we were heading for a major conflict.

It came when Micah flew off into a rage one day. He was slamming doors and cursing, and I felt the protective mama bear rise up within me. No way was I going to expose my babies to behavior like this, especially because I knew that for some of them the sound of shouting and the threat of violence would likely remind them of painful memories in their own lives. So I calmly knocked on the door that Micah had slammed and told him that he could not stay with us any longer.

He left the next day. It didn't take long before we noticed an improvement in the behavior of the other four. Still, it did not feel like we were a good fit for them. They had known such independence and lived so long without being a part of a family that it was too hard for them to unlearn old habits of doing whatever they wanted whenever they wanted. Pierre-Richard and I prayed for guidance as well as grace, and we were convinced that in time Fito, Julmis, Stenio, and Fabienne would leave us as well.

After a few weeks of them staying with us, the man who had first phoned us to ask for help paid us a visit. We didn't talk about how the young men were getting along with the family. There wasn't time. Almost as soon as he arrived and spoke with the four of them, he announced that they were all going to be leaving soon.

"They've been offered a chance to live in Nicaragua," he said. It was a surprise but not unheard of. Haiti had good links with South and Central American countries, and each year plenty of Haitians leave with the hope of starting a new life in countries like Peru and Nicaragua. If there was a chance of starting over in a new country with the support of a local nonprofit, maybe it was just what they all needed. "Stenio's going with them, too, and it's easier for us to apply for visas in the Dominican Republic, so I'm going to take them all to live there and wait while the paperwork comes through."

We prayed together, talked about what they might expect, and sent them off with our blessing. Life in the compound returned to something like normal.

We heard nothing from them for almost six months. And then, another unexpected phone call came.

"Mama? It's Julmis."

It took me a moment to collect my thoughts. He sounded different. He sounded young. "It's really you, Julmis? Where are you?"

"Port-au-Prince."

"What happened to going to Nicaragua?"

His voice grew even quieter. "We didn't go. We were refused a visa."

"I'm sorry to hear that. How are you?"

"Bad, Mama. Stenio and I have been staying with a family, but they're not treating us well."

I asked him what he meant, and he described a situation that sounded so familiar it made me flinch. Without any family or education, the two boys had faced a choice of going back on the streets or finding a family to take them in. They chose family, but like hundreds of thousands of others in their situation across Haiti, they were treated pretty much like slaves. I thought back to the *restavecs* we used to stare at when we were kids running around Port-au-Prince. They were the out-of-towners, the ones we pitied. However bad our own lives were, we'd say at least we weren't a *restavec*.

But the biggest surprise of that day was still to come. "Mama," said Julmis, "can we come back to live with you?"

When Pierre-Richard and I prayed later that day, we both knew that God was inviting us to welcome the brothers back. We could have said no, but we didn't want to. We both sensed that something had changed in them and that it was right for them to return.

Within a week, Julmis and Stenio were back, but they were so different. Gone was the sense that Julmis was impatient to be somewhere else or the feeling that family life was beneath him. Gone was the Stenio who would not talk. In their place were a Julmis and Stenio who were polite, respectful, and kind. They quickly became as much a part of us as any of our other children.

Almost as soon as they returned, we heard from Fito and Fabienne. Even though they had all been scattered around Haiti, each of them had experienced a similarly difficult few months. They'd all ended up living as *restavecs,* and they all wanted to come home.

Fabienne had never been anything but polite and wonderful when she first stayed with us, so there was no real change in her. She was the same model of respect and dignity she always had been. But Fito had undergone a transformation as dramatic as had Julmis and Stenio.

There was one slight problem we had to overcome when they returned. All of them were so far behind in their education. We were clear with them that if they were going to live with us, they needed to complete their schooling all the way through to the end. They agreed, although for Fito it was a particularly tough decision. He was 20 years old but had never passed sixth grade.

"Look," he said, showing me his certificate, "I'm in ninth grade."

I smiled. He could barely read what was written on the certificate, let alone sit for the exams at the end of eighth grade. "Honey, I know what's happened. You missed so much school, but they let you pay to get the certificate each year. Am I right?"

He swallowed, looked kind of shocked, then nodded.

"You've got to complete sixth grade, Fito. It's the platform that all the rest of your schooling gets built on. If you can't do the basics you learn in sixth grade, everything that comes next is going to be so much harder."

Fito cried.

Eventually he dried his face and said that he would do what we suggested. His courage impressed me so much. If ever I doubted how much Fito and the others had changed, I only have to look at him studying and working hard alongside children half his size. His determination and his humility never fail to inspire me.

A few weeks ago, Fito stood in front of all his brothers and sisters—quite a crowd these days—and listened to their cheers as they celebrated his final day at high school. Tears poured down his face, and it took him a while before he could speak.

"I never dreamed that I would finish school," he said. "I always thought I could not learn."

. . . .

Even though we never heard from Micah and would have loved to see what God was doing in his life, Pierre-Richard and I were so glad to welcome the four others home. Though, if I'm honest, it was probably a little easier for Pierre-Richard than for me. My husband is kind and loving and the most forgiving person I've ever met. He's driven by compassion and motivated by love (closely followed by good food). He's soft, gentle, and will open his heart again and again to anyone. I'm a strong person who doesn't like to change her mind once it has been made up. So while Pierre-Richard was ready to welcome each of them back within seconds, I had some work to do.

When they left the first time, I assumed that it was a confirmation of God's plan. It made sense to me that they were only supposed to be with us for a short time, and I trusted that although it had not worked out well with Micah, God would use the time we spent with them for His plans and His purposes.

Seeing Julmis, Stenio, Fito, and Fabienne return and fit so easily into family life taught me a valuable lesson. God reveals the parts of His plans that He wants to reveal at the time that He wants to reveal them. We cannot predict or plot where or how He will work, so we have to hold lightly to anything He gives us. But what is also true is that while God's plans are above and beyond our understanding, there is never a time to withhold grace, mercy, and forgiveness. We might not know what lies ahead, but we can still choose to face whatever situation we find ourselves in with love and second chances.

It wasn't just the four kids who changed. I did too. In accepting them home, I was making a choice not as a director of a school, but as a mother. I was following Pierre-Richard's lead and acting as a parent. Above all else, I was choosing to love.

It felt intuitive and right to behave in this way, but it was still a big step for me. To choose to act as a parent instead of a program director meant making myself vulnerable. It's easy to hide behind rules and systems, practices and procedures. After all, it's what I'd done at Fonds Baillard. But here, on our compound, I wanted to make a different choice—to love, to forgive, and to put aside the rules in pursuit of the relationship.

Julmis, Stenio, Fito, and Fabienne had taught me something profound. By humbling themselves, they made it possible for me to follow their lead. They behaved like children—children who go in search of a loving adult to care for them and protect them. I could see why they thought they might find that in Pierre-Richard, but me too? That was the most humbling thing of all.

Slowly it began to dawn on me that becoming Mama wasn't about a single event that changed me. I didn't become a mama in one simple, single event. It wasn't a case of God saving me from the earthquake or having Luckmane say that he wanted to live with us. It was the journey of a thousand steps, each one a lesson carefully planned by God alone.

Psalm 139 says it best:

> For you formed my inward parts;
>   you knitted me together in my mother's womb.
> I praise you, for I am fearfully and wonderfully made.

Wonderful are your works;
my soul knows it very well (verses 13-14).

God made me a mama the same way He made me His child: fiber by fiber, moment by moment. His care and His love never fail to astound me, and I am forever grateful to Him for such incredible kindness and care.

. . . .

The return of our four prodigals introduced something new to family life. When they came back, the children who had been with us all along needed to talk about it. We started having conversations as part of our morning and night time prayer and worship sessions, and each time there was a tangible sense of God being present as the children asked questions freely.

"Where did you go?"

"Why did you come back?"

"Are you glad you're here?"

Our children amazed me. They were so like their pappy, full of love and grace and warmth. They listened to the answers they received, and each time we'd embrace and thank God for putting us in this wonderful family.

Today, whenever a new child joins us or if there is something that needs to be said, these times of prayer and worship are when the conversations take place. No matter how long we've been living together, we ask God to help us confess, to help us forgive, and to help us grow strong together. He never lets us down.

. . . .

Julmis, Stenio, Fito, and Fabienne have stayed with us ever since their return. Fabienne dedicated herself to working hard at her studies and thrived at high school—thanks to endless hours of support from Pierre-Richard. The three boys are all growing up to become strong, respectful, kind, and loving men. They are wonderful role models for so many of our younger boys, and not a day goes by without Pierre-Richard and I thanking God for bringing them into our family.

Their return sparked one more change. We had been able to accommodate them when they stayed with us the first time, but when they came back, it was clear that with so many children now in our family, we were running out of room. The two rooms that we rented had long since reached capacity, and the older children were scattered among the tents and five metal buildings that Pastor Rod Baker had constructed across our compound. It was obvious that something needed to change, and we even had a sense that God had a plan in the works. I remembered the old dreams from the days when I first met Marie, and I focused on one detail that I had overlooked at the time: a house, broad and wide and tall, big enough to fit all of us with room to spare.

This was no fantasy house. It was real, and I had seen it. In fact, it had already been built by the wonderful Bill Montgomery. Bill had bought two plots of land right next to ours. One plot he gave to us, and the other he kept for himself. One summer, some of his construction friends came from the U.S. and put up the house he was going to live in soon. It was strong and solid, with two big rooms downstairs on either side of a large meeting space. Up above was a beautiful, open room with views of the lake at the front and the mountains at the rear.

It was a beautiful house that I knew would be perfect for us. There were just two problems: Bill wasn't selling, and even if he was, no way could we afford to buy the house.

15

WELCOME HOME

B ill's selling."
I stopped pumping water into my bucket and looked up at Pastor Rod. He raised his eyes and smiled. "That's right. He's decided to move."

I was amazed. I had no idea that he was planning anything like this. As far as I knew, Bill was staying. He'd bought the land right next to ours, built his house, and was using it as a base for his mission work. Since the UN had set up their office in the town, other nonprofits and good causes had chosen Fond Parisien as their base of operation. It was a great location on a well-maintained road, right by the border with the Dominican Republic. It was close enough to Port-au-Prince to get into the city quickly, yet far enough away to be free from its chaos. There was a growing number of people like Bill in the town, missionaries from the U.S. who had heard the call of God to come and work in Haiti.

Part of me felt sad at the news. Bill was like one of those kindly uncles in a family movie. With his white hair and beard, his ability to fix anything with his hands and all his training in farming and construction, he was someone we relied on. He gave us food regularly, and he had even built the water pump that I was using. Without Bill as our neighbor, life in Fond Parisien would be different. I was not sure that I was ready.

"Yvrose, I think you should buy it."

I looked at Pastor Rod and laughed. I couldn't even afford to pay the salaries of the eight teachers we employed to teach the 400 pupils enrolled at our school. Every few months, Pierre-Richard and I went through the same cycle of praying desperately to God, pleading with Him to intervene and then watching, amazed, for the way that He prompted someone to give. Yes, it was a privilege to live like this and be so dependent on God, but praying in a few hundred dollars was nothing compared to the tens of thousands it would cost to buy a house like Bill's.

Pierre-Richard and I talked and prayed a lot. Neither of us could see how we would ever be able to raise enough money to buy a whole house, especially when we heard from Bill that, yes, he really was selling, and the price would be $60,000.

We were so out of our depth it wasn't even funny. No bank would lend us the money, and none of our supporters had ever given anything close to this amount. We were powerless, in need, and desperate for God to help. We also had a small but growing hope that God might in some way step in. We were exactly where He wanted us.

We should have known that God would surprise us. And He did—quickly, and in the most spectacular way.

First, Pastor Rod gave us a check for $20,000. Then, a friend from back in the U.S. visited us. We purposefully didn't say anything to her about the house, but within a day of her arrival, she sat Pierre-Richard and me down. "Listen, I heard Bill's house is for sale.

You need to know that God has been speaking to my heart that I should help you buy it."

Three days later, she gave me a check for $30,000.

My church in Nantucket heard about the house and told us that they were going to fund-raise too. Then we had a similar message from the church in Bolney, England. Within the space of a few weeks, we reached $70,000—enough to cover the purchase price as well as all the legal fees and taxes.

God had done it without us. We hadn't fund-raised or gone out and tried to make our case to people. In fact, we hadn't done anything much more than pray and open our hands to receive the gifts that He prompted people to give. It was a lesson in trusting Him that would change us in significant ways.

Moving into the house in 2013 marked the beginning of something new for us. It was a relief and a blessing that we finally had enough room for each of our 32 children to have a bed, but the house made something else possible as well. In the open-sided room at the top of the house, we had the potential to accommodate visitors who wanted to come and stay. With a balcony overlooking the lake, and the mountains reaching high up into the skies behind, it was the perfect place for visitors to sleep, rest, and soak in all the good things they could see God doing in our compound below.

God has always brought the right people along at the right time. From the first days of meeting Marie to the arrival of Bill, from the help of old friends from the U.S. to that of new friends from England, God has proved Himself faithful in so many ways.

When we have worried about the health of some of our children, He has brought doctors to visit. When we have needed help improving the way the school is run, He has brought teachers. And when we have needed people to help us on mission trips to remote areas of the country, He has brought men and women of God who said yes to every adventure He laid before them.

As much as these visits have blessed us, we have had the joy of seeing how those that come are blessed too. One doctor who came to spend time with us was so moved that she ended up adopting a little girl she met in Port-au-Prince. Others have heard the call to return to Haiti and become missionaries here, setting up projects unrelated to us. More than once, we've been asked whether this would be okay, as if this little corner of Haiti is our domain or we have the power to grant permission. To each of them, Pierre-Richard and I have said, "Come! There's so much need here, and we'll happily show you where it is." If they want to set up their own thing, how could we do anything but celebrate their obedience and God's goodness?

Not everyone who visits us knows why they are here. Some come without knowing their purpose, unsure of what God's calling is on their lives. Some come without even knowing who God is. I love when this happens, because even though you never know how or when God is going to act, His presence is so tangible that it gets right to the heart.

One day a group from outside Seattle came to stay on a mission trip. Most of them were from church, but one of the young men had no background there and no faith to speak of. He was a good guy with arms covered in tattoos.

"You like my dragon?" he asked when he saw me looking at his arms.

I nodded and smiled.

"It's my protection," he said.

"That's interesting," I said. "The One we're serving here is the creator of that dragon."

He looked confused at first, then said something I didn't expect at all.

"I don't want you to judge me."

"Why would I judge you? God sent you here. I always pray that

God will only send us the people who He is going to use as an instrument for Him. So if God sends you and you come, I'm pretty sure that means He's got a plan for you. He's inviting you to say yes to Him. I don't have any desire to judge you at all. I'm just excited for what God might be about to do through you."

I remembered what it was like when I first arrived in Fonds Baillard. The poverty was shocking enough to force me right out of my comfort zone. "When you see a smile on the face of someone who has nothing, you realize that they have something you don't," I added. "Jesus was always found around the poor, and it's still the same today. When you spend time with people who have nothing physically but who know God's love in a deep, deep way, it rubs off on you."

School ended then and the compound erupted with the sound of hundreds of happy children celebrating the end of another week of lessons. Our conversation ended, but over the rest of the week, I prayed repeatedly that God would have His way and speak clearly to this brave young man who had taken a risk to visit us.

Through years of having people come, we've discovered a profound and simple truth: When you trust God, your appetite for God increases. And when that happens, you get led into all kinds of things. Coming to a place where God is clearly at work draws you closer to God.

I've shared these words with so many people. While some have become Christians while they are with us, others have gone home without our knowing what happened next. But I know for sure that for every person who visits, there is an opportunity to meet God. Not because of anything that Pierre-Richard and I are doing, but simply because of God Himself. Wherever the poor are, that's where He'll often be most clearly at work.

· · · · · · · · · · · ·

As a result of being able to welcome so many people into our home, the school started to grow rapidly. When we bought the house from Bill in 2013, we had 400 students enrolled. Within two years, that number had grown to 600.

With so many pupils, the needs are great, but when people ask us if they can send us some items instead of coming in person, I always tell them, "Bringing yourself instead of sending money or school supplies is so much better for all of us. When people visit, they make relationships. They see God at work and sometimes—often, in fact—they hear God. Maybe it's because they're free from the pressures of normal life, or maybe it's just because we have bad internet here. I don't know why, but I do know that God has spoken clearly to many of our visitors. Some He has told to support us, others He has sent away with different passions burning within them. In every situation we rejoice, happy that God continues to allow us to play a small part in His plans."

Not every part of this was easy for me. Of course, it was easy to be happy that people were hearing from God, but directly asking people to visit? That was tough. I still had a whole load of baggage to work through, and at the top of the pile was the fear that people would find fault in what I was doing, see me at my worst, and think badly of me.

After the earthquake, God had so clearly revealed to me where I had gone wrong before. I had relied on my 401(k) and my own strength. I wasn't humble; I was proud. I wanted to be seen as the kind of person who could shoulder all the responsibility that God gave her. I wanted to show no weakness.

I still experience the temptation to work in my own strength rather than reach out to God. It's a struggle I face, and I know that I must regularly check my motives for responding to certain situations. But God's message to me remains the same: *Let Me do it. And when you do, look how much stronger things grow.*

• • • • • • • • • • • •

When you have a lot of children and not much money, certain things are easy to ask for. Food. Clothes. Shoes. School supplies. These are the kinds of gifts that people like to bring. Bedsheets? Not so much. Who could ever get excited about handing out those?

I'd been praying, trying to figure out a way of raising money for sheets when we were asked whether we could host a group of young people from a church in Atlanta. We had met them the year before when they visited a project nearby. We liked them and were happy to have them stay with us.

One morning after we finished praying and worshipping, the leader whispered to me that they wanted to do something nice for our kids in the afternoon.

"We need an hour," she said. "Can you let us have the house on our own for that time?"

I agreed, then didn't think much more about it. That afternoon Pierre-Richard and I took the children down to the soccer pitch, which was the first strip of land that Pierre-Richard bought me as an engagement present. The old container that the church in Nantucket had shipped us following the earthquake was still there. If I closed my eyes, I could easily remember what it looked like when we tied the tarp to the container's corners and pitched our two little tents underneath—Baby and Rosekencia with me in one, Luckmane and Ricardo with Pierre-Richard in the other. In many ways, much had changed since then. We had a house and a water pump. We had proper beds and changes of clothes and charcoal on which to cook. But some things remained the same. We were still in need. We were still way out of our depth and unable to make any of this work in our own strength. We were still reliant on God, and for that I was so thankful.

The hour ended and one of the young people from Atlanta ran down from the house and found us.

"Miss Yvrose? Would y'all come back now?"

I had guessed what they were going to do. They were going to cook us a meal or make s'mores or set up the house so that the kids could have a party. I was wrong.

"We had a competition," said the leader. "We wanted to see which team could do the best room makeover."

What they had done took my breath away and brought tears to my eyes. Each of the bedrooms had been cleaned, then made over in the most amazing ways. There were flowers, cushions, and throws. And on every bed, in every bedroom, there were beautiful, brand-new bedsheets.

I looked at my children. Their faces were wet with their own tears, their smiles as wide as I'd ever seen them. They stared, stunned and silent.

"Wait," said the leader as she held my hand, her smile as wide as anyone's. "Come with me."

I had assumed they were only going to make over the kids' rooms, but she opened the door to my and Pierre-Richard's bedroom. I walked in, half expecting to see the usual pile of suitcases full of school supplies, spare clothes, and everything else we squeeze by our bedside. Instead, I saw a beautiful space. They had carefully organized all the supplies in one corner of the room and made the rest look stunning. There were flowers and throws and cushions, and fresh linens on the bed.

"How did you know?"

She looked at me like I had asked her how she traveled from Atlanta to Haiti, or how the sun rose in the sky every morning, as if it was the most obvious question anyone could ever ask.

"The Lord told us, Yvrose. That's how."

That night we worshipped and prayed and thanked God—loudly

and long. We danced and sang until our feet were sore and our voices hoarse.

As I crept into my bed that night and felt the cool linen beneath my fingers, I whispered my prayer to God. "Thank You, Lord. Thank You. You gave all of us such a wonderful gift today. But I believe it's more than bedsheets and throws that You've given. You've shown us again that we can trust You for the things we want but don't know how to ask for."

· · · · · · · · · · · · ·

Some time after we bought Bill's house and started receiving visits from groups, we realized that we needed a name for what we were doing here, both the school and our family. There was only one word we could think of that would be suitable, a word that was at the heart of everything we are doing: *hope*. So the school became known as Hope Christian Academy and our home as Hope House Haiti. We grew a little bigger. We took on more teachers. We registered as a charity in England and as a nonprofit in the U.S. We have had more visitors.

But some things did not change. When people ask what we need, I always say exactly the same thing.

"Prayer."

It's not that I'm avoiding asking for specific things or that I'm worried people will be offended if what I ask for costs more than they had in mind to spend. I ask for prayer because without it, we're lost.

Sometimes people push back a little. "But what do you *need*? There must be something we can bring that will be of value."

There are always things I could tell them, and at any point I can run through a long list that begins with food and hygiene items and clothes, and then goes all the way up to an extra half acre of land and the building supplies required to construct a new school building or house. But I don't go there. I don't want to be the one who sets the priorities. I want God to be in charge, not me. So, if someone persists and really wants to know what they can bring, I tell them to pray some more. "Pray that God speaks to you about what we need. He knows what we need better than we do."

In the same way that we are a family and not an orphanage, I don't want us to be a nonprofit that is run like a business. We're built on hope; we're created to trust God for all our needs. We're here to listen to Him and encourage others to do the same.

· · · · · · · · · · · · ·

When I look around our home and the school, I can see so many things I would like to do. We could buy many different things that would greatly improve life. But I have given up trying to work out what is a want and what is a need. I tried for a while, but it's so confusing. And life is easier when you leave it to God to decide what we really, truly need.

I love God's sense of humor. The group from Atlanta has returned every year. They fix up the little boys' and girls' rooms—and always bring sheets. It never fails to make us all smile, and I only have to look at any of the many beds in our house to be reminded of God's kindness and love.

It's the same with my shoes.

I used to love buying shoes. I'd plan my purchases and coordinate my outfits. And if someone looked at a new pair I had on and told me they wanted a pair just like them, I'd feel a warm glow inside that would stay with me for an hour at least.

Shoes definitely became an idol for me.

When I moved to Haiti, I left nearly all my shoes behind, giving them away to friends in Charlotte. I brought only my favorites with me, but even they felt wrong somehow. One day I took them down with me to church, plus a few dresses that I had, and told people they could take whatever they wanted.

The freedom I felt lasted for days.

But God was not done with me and my feet. A month later, we had a team visit us. They brought with them a suitcase full of shoes. There were shoes for the boys and shoes for the girls, all good and practical school shoes and sneakers. But at the bottom of the case were ten pairs of fancy-looking heels that nobody could fit into. Nobody except me.

Now God and I have a game together. It's called *Who Can Give the Most?* I try my best, sharing the shoes and giving away our food so that we only ever have enough for the next day. We open the tall metal gates of the compound and invite anyone who wants water to come and use our pump without charge.

But no matter how much we give away, God always gives more. When it comes to generosity, He's impossible to beat.

16

THE POWERS OF DARKNESS

I t's not easy reaching the remote village communities high in the mountains behind our compound. It takes hours of bouncing along rocky tracks on the back of a motorbike, followed by a few more hours on the back of a donkey—both along crumbling, narrow paths beside steep drops down to the ravine below. Finally, there's another hour or two on foot, scrambling over rocks. But after nearly a full day of travel to reach the most remote locations, it's worthwhile. The air is cooler, the vegetation dense, and, in some ways, it feels like another country completely.

And yes, sadly, almost all of the problems that affect people living in the slums and the cities are also problems for the mountain communities. Poverty and lack of access to education and other services are all challenges we encounter whenever Pierre-Richard and I head up to the mountains, often with visitors who want to involve themselves in missions. We take food and bring medical teams when we can. In 2012, we even helped set up a new school for people living in a remote mountain area a few hours away from Fond Parisien. But if there's one problem that troubles me more than all the others, it is this: witchcraft.

Our connection with the mountain villages started when we met Wilner, Julbert, and Celicia, not long after we moved to Fond Parisien. After they came to live with us, we continued to make regular journeys to the area to deliver food, talk about Jesus, and build relationships with the families. And it was on one of these early trips that we heard a story that troubled us greatly about a family there.

According to the rumor, the grandmother of the family practiced voodoo. She served a particular spirit and knew that since she was getting old she needed to initiate someone else to take her place when she died. The old woman had decided that her six-year-old granddaughter was the chosen one and made preparations to hand her over into a life of service to this dark, satanic force.

The girl didn't want to be initiated. The grandmother pressured her to agree to the ceremony, but the girl held out. But a six-year-old girl is no match for a voodoo priestess, and the grandmother pushed ahead with plans for the ceremony. That's when the little girl went missing.

For three days, she survived by eating grass. She didn't go far but stayed close to the village, partly in the hope that someone would help her, partly because she wanted to watch what was going on. To prevent herself from being discovered, she concentrated on making herself invisible, willing anyone who walked near the pile of leaves where she was hiding to keep on walking by.

Eventually, she was found and taken back to the family home.

As soon as we heard this story, we wanted to meet the family. Nobody could tell us where they lived or even what their names were, so we prayed that God would guide us. It was hard waiting for news. We had no idea whether the grandmother had succeeded in her plans for the little girl, or whether there had been further escapes. We prayed harder, and sure enough, God stepped in. A few months after we heard the story, we were told that the father wanted to meet us.

"This is my son," he said when we were finally introduced to him. "I want you to take him to your school."

"Your son?" I was confused. Nobody had ever said anything about a son before.

"Yes, I want you to give him an education, but I cannot afford any fees."

"Well, we might be able to do that, but I hear you have a daughter living with you."

"Two."

"Two daughters? And have they ever attended school?"

He brushed my question away as if it was a mosquito. "There's no need."

"Excuse me, sir, but there is. There's such a great need for girls to be educated." He didn't look convinced, so I tried another argument. "If you send your girls to the school, I'll take your son as well. No fees for any of them."

He looked at me, hard and cold. "I will come and see you." He took his son and turned to leave.

"Can I meet your daughters? I'd like to see them."

"No. They're out working."

I asked when they would be home, but his hand waved me off again as he turned his back on me, shuffling away.

A few weeks later we were returning home from a trip to Port-au-Prince when I saw the man's son and a young girl sitting on the step at the front of the house. As soon as I reached them, the others started talking excitedly.

"Their father brought them while you were out," said Pierre-Richard's mother, who was now living with us. The girl was tiny, maybe only four or five years old. I guessed she was not the one the grandmother had wanted to initiate. I was angry. I hated getting played like this.

The little girl looked terrified, so I sat down beside her. "What's your name, precious?"

"Eliana."

Eliana didn't stay timid for long. By the end of the day, she was smiling and helping out alongside the other kids. It was obvious that she was smart, and we knew that letting her and her brother, Nacius, enroll at school was the right thing to do. The older sister—who we found out was called Sonita—was still at home. We decided that we would just have to trust God for her safety, and if the time was right, God would bring her to us.

A few weeks later, God did exactly that. Nacius and Eliana went home for a few days. When they returned, Sonita was with them. She joined the school and, like her sister and brother, lived with us.

It took a long time for Sonita to tell us more about what happened with her grandmother, and even now I'm not sure we've ever really heard the whole story. But Sonita, Nacius, and Eliana have all decided to follow Jesus. They are prayerful, bold, faithful disciples, and they each know and trust God to protect them.

A little over a year ago, their father came to the house.

"Your grandmother is dying," he said. "You must come back with me to see her."

Nacius spoke first. "No. I'm not going."

"Nor am I," said Sonita.

"Not me," said Eliana.

Their dad stared at them with a mixture of shock and anger.

"They are followers of Jesus now," I said calmly. "Are you surprised they don't want to go back to witchcraft?"

He shrugged and left.

Their grandmother died soon after, and when we heard the news, I reassured the three children that they had made the right decision.

"Are you sure?"

"Yes," I told them. "You don't know what plans God might have for you in the future. Maybe one day you will return to the mountains and take the gospel to them."

. . . .

Everyone in Haiti is aware of the prevalence of voodoo, and we all know it is nothing like the hokey tourist kitsch that some people like to pretend it is. Through voodoo, the power of darkness is great, but the power of God to overcome it and turn lives around is greater still. I can say this with total assurance because I have seen it with my own eyes. Even in the L'Artibonite region—an area infamous for being the hub of much satanic activity—I have seen God at work.

Once you head north from Port-au-Prince and travel up the west coast, you'll soon see the familiar roadside shrines marking the area as a voodoo hot spot. But it's at night when the sun goes down that the real darkness emerges. People will gather on the street, dressed all in white and carry out voodoo ceremonies. If strangers wander in, there's a chance they won't ever make it out alive.

I have taken visitors there only a handful of times. We prayed long and hard beforehand and only went when we were sure we were going with God's blessing and protection. Even so, those trips left me with lasting memories.

One time I had taken two Christian girls from the U.S. We left Fond Parisien early one morning and were able to spend the afternoon visiting a village where my brother had worked previously. Pastor Jean showed a Creole version of the *Jesus* movie, then we gave out food and water and talked with many different people about Jesus. Because the roads in Haiti are unsafe to drive on at night, we lay down on our sleeping mats outside a broken-down house that my brother had told us was safe. Then we heard drums and the chanting of at least a dozen voices.

My two companions looked at me. Something in my face must have set them off, because they both started praying immediately. The louder the drums grew, the clearer the voices became. The crowd came close, and the chanting and drumming got so loud that we were all praying out loud at the top of our voices and still couldn't always hear ourselves.

One of the girls screamed and pointed at a man, dressed in white like all voodoo worshippers, who had run into where we were camped, grabbed her bag, and run off. Acting more on instinct than anything else, the three of us chased after him. It was no use. He knew the village and we didn't.

Back at the broken-down house, we prayed for hours, pleading with God to return the bag that was full of cash, passports, and a phone, plus various medications, glasses, and credit cards. We stayed awake, praying until our heads grew heavy and we drifted off to sleep.

The next day was Sunday. We went to church, still praying for God to intervene. Before the service was over, someone had told us that the bag had been found, although without the cash or cell phone. This allowed us to share the Gospel with a bunch of people, which was a small victory that we thanked God for, but we left knowing that the people in L'Artibonite had a desperate need to hear the good news of Jesus.

Months later, some of our friends from England were with us, including a number of pastors. We prayed and again felt like God gave us permission to go, so we left Fond Parisien early in the morning, ready to spend 24 hours praying, helping, and talking to people living in darkness about the Light of the World.

Something felt different from the moment we reached the village, as if the air was somehow thicker or the gravity stronger. We took it as a sign that something beyond our understanding was happening and trusted that God would get us through whatever He had called us into.

The first woman we met stunned us.

She was younger than me, looked timid, and had a weariness about her that I'd seen in other people caught up in voodoo.

"I used to be a Christian," she told us as we sheltered ourselves under the shade of a palm tree. "But I need you to pray for me."

We nodded. "Of course we will. Is there anything specific you would like us to pray about."

The woman looked at us for a while, weighing whether to say more. "Yes," she said eventually, dropping her voice so much that we both had to lean in close to hear. "I stopped being a Christian and started following the spirits. I took part in a ceremony when someone gave me a snake, and I let it go inside me."

At first, I struggled to absorb what she was saying. It was almost too much to understand. But as we talked some more and she explained how there were times when she was convinced she could feel the snake still living inside her, we both knew that we were way out of our depth. Only God could help.

We prayed. Not for long, and not too loud either. But with quiet authority—plus a lot of silent pleading to God to help—we spoke our words of truth into the air. "The power of God is greater than the power of darkness…the blood of Christ can wash away any sin…in the name of Jesus we break whatever chains have been placed on this woman."

She rededicated her life to God, and we knew we were finished when a familiar peace settled on us. The woman told us she felt better and thought the snake was finally gone.

We saw her the next day, right before we left. She looked ten years younger and full of energy.

"Gone?" I asked.

"Gone!" She smiled. "And my husband gave his life to God this morning too!"

Our visits to the villages brought us into contact with other Christians through whom God was working. Some were locals, others from overseas. None had a story as remarkable as Martine, a young woman in her twenties whom we met when she spoke at a church we visited.

Martine didn't know what happened to her parents, but she thinks she was two years old when she was taken in by a voodoo priest. She remembers the man telling her something she would never forget: "On your third birthday, I'm going to give you the best present of all."

The day she turned three, Martine was taken to a voodoo ceremony where she was initiated to serve Lucifer himself. From that day on, she grew up knowing that she had a single mission in her life: to kill.

By the time she was 13 years old, Martine had started killing. She had power to cause accidents, power to control people to make them do things they never normally would do. And for years she didn't eat food. Human blood was all she needed.

Martine knew she would die before she turned 18, and as she entered the final years of her life, she took on a new mission: to seduce and kill Christian pastors. She'd visit churches and pretend to be interested in converting. She'd strike up a relationship with the pastor and, eventually, kill him.

She was desperate to catch one pastor. She'd heard that he was a man of stronger faith than most. So, when Martine heard that he was due to visit her region and preach for a week, she fasted from blood for days, took a friend with her, and visited one of his meetings. She tried the same routine she had used before—weeping at the front, asking for forgiveness, saying she wanted to be saved—only this time, the temperature in the church was so hot that she had to get out. She smoked a whole pack of cigarettes in minutes, then went back in.

"Young woman coming in right now," said the pastor, pointing right at her. "The Lord told me about you some time ago, and He sent me for you. Today is your day of salvation. The devil doesn't really have a grip on you. You are not going to die before you are 18. God is ready for you."

She fell down. She was desperate not to fail her mission, knowing that she would be brutally punished if she did. She wept harder than ever and slowly approached the front. As soon as the pastor put his hand on her forehead, she fell again. Many thoughts ran through her mind, and her fear of Lucifer was great. But the Light was stronger. The call of Jesus was louder. The love that she had never known existed was undeniable. It was to God she turned that day, and God alone.

. . . .

Not long after I met Martine and heard her story, I woke up one night, agitated. I couldn't settle and knew that I needed to go outside and pray around the compound. I felt a pull toward the area where we taught the kids under a tarp, and I prayed all around it.

I called Marie the next day and asked her to pray too.

"Of course," she said. "What are we praying about, exactly?"

"I don't know," I said. "All I know for sure is that we need to pray."

Two days later, I was in the house after school had finished when the lady who cleaned came to find me.

"Madame Ismael, I found something you should come look at."

I followed her to the space we used as a kindergarten. As soon as we walked around the back, I could smell it—a strange scent that I'd only ever smelled in Haiti. Like rancid perfume and hot pepper got mixed together and burned. I felt sick, but not because of the smell itself. What troubled me was the fact that I knew the smell could only mean one thing.

"Look there," said the lady, pointing to a pile of items on the ground.

Any Haitian would recognize them. The blue paint on the ground, packages wrapped up in brightly colored but faded cloth. Old glass bottles and bones and the remnants of a small fire. Someone had been performing voodoo ceremonies here in the school. And not just in any classroom, but the kindergarten—the place where our youngest, most vulnerable children were looked after.

I felt faint. It was hard to breathe. My head spun, and I needed to sit down on one of the benches. I knew there were people in Fond Parisien who practiced witchcraft—there wasn't a town in Haiti that voodoo hadn't reached. Even though Pierre-Richard and I still had regular visits from the local voodoo priest, I knew instinctively that it wouldn't have been him who broke in and performed the ceremony here. But who else could it be? I ran through a list in my mind. It could have been anyone, likely someone I didn't know. We made no secret of our faith in Jesus, so we were an obvious target.

"Madame Ismael," said the cleaning lady, putting her hand on my shoulder. "I told the school director about this first."

I tried to shake the haze from my head. "Okay. And what did he say?"

"He told me to clear it up..." She caught herself, the words stuck in her throat.

"What is it?"

"He told me not to tell you about it."

17

JABETTA

I was 25 years old on the day I first thought I was about to die. I'd known fear before then, and all those visits to the doctor when I was pregnant had led me to worry that if I carried on, one day I would wind up dead. But the day I ran through the streets of Port-au-Prince, chased by armed men, was the moment I first assumed that my life had only minutes left. As soon as they found me, I knew they'd kill me.

It had been coming for a while. When Baby Doc Duvalier took over from his ruthless tyrant of a father, he had his henchmen and security services track down any individuals who posed a threat. And there was no greater threat than our priest, Jean-Bertrand Aristide. Simply knowing him put us at risk, but my siblings and I were more than parishioners or acquaintances. We were revolutionaries ready to serve alongside him and do all we could to rid our homeland of its dictator. Because of this, my siblings and I were on an official list of undesirables. I'd managed to avoid getting caught for weeks, but I knew it was only a matter of time before they caught me. And, on the day I was walking in the city and heard a car's brakes screaming as it slammed to a halt behind me, I was ready to run.

I was fast and young, but one look behind me revealed that my three pursuers were strong and armed. My only hope was to lose them, and for that I needed to get off the streets wide enough for cars to drive down and into the narrow warren of the slums. Trouble was, I was nowhere near my home slum of Fort Nationale. All I could do was turn down the nearest side street and hope for the best.

My pursuers did not shout or scream. They ran in silence, chasing me down like hunters. I slammed into walls and pushed myself through crowds of people. I ran down alleys I had never seen before, hoping they would realize that catching me was a lost cause and would give up. Only when I thought I had lost them did I allow myself to slow just a little and look back.

Dumb mistake. As I turned around, one of my pursuers turned the corner. He was looking right at me, 40 feet away. Our eyes met, and he surged toward me.

I ran, taking every turn that I could. I was frantically pushing myself down alleys and around the backs of shacks, willing my feet to move faster and my legs and lungs to ignore the pain searing through them.

Something caught my foot, and I slammed down onto the ground. A new shock of pain ran through my leg. I'd tripped over a length of wood that stuck out from a pile of building materials at the side of a house. My knee was pouring blood and my head felt cold. I started to push myself up when I heard voices gasping for breath behind me.

"She's close. Find her."

I looked up. Nowhere to go. The alley was blocked off up ahead and there were no doors to force open. The only thing nearby was an old sack on the pile of rubble. I pulled it over me, wondering how many seconds I would have before they pulled off my desperate disguise.

I heard footsteps approaching. I could picture the men standing at the end of the alley, looking in my direction. Slowly, one of them approached. Each step brought him closer to me. I closed my eyes and took what I was sure were going to be my final breaths.

God saved me that day. I understood that right away. As soon as the footsteps faded and I peeled back the sack, I knew that whatever had just happened was some kind of divine intervention. But it took me years, even decades, before I finally began to appreciate what God was teaching me through it.

For the longest time I lived my life like I was running away from my pursuers. Whenever I faced a danger or a threat, I responded in my own strength. I took matters into my own hands, made my own plans, and hoped that if I just kept going, I'd win out. It took the earthquake and the hurricane to remind me that what I really needed to do was lie down, stop running, and trust God for protection.

* * * * * * * * * * * *

Soon after we found the voodoo tools at the school, five teachers (including the school director) left us. We never knew for sure, but the timing led us to assume that they had all been working to bring evil into our school. It hurled us into the biggest crisis we had ever encountered. We had hundreds of students we couldn't teach, and finding replacement staff was almost impossible. I could feel the danger closing in behind us.

But I'd finally learned my lesson. Instead of trying to fix it myself, I turned to God. I didn't run; I got to my knees and turned to Him for protection. It might sound odd to praise God when it seems as though there's no hope, but it works. Reminding ourselves that He's always there is how we keep our hope alive.

So many times, when opposition threatens us or our needs become overwhelming, I gather the children together in a corner and pray. We look at the Bible and remind ourselves just how faithful God is. We sing loud and long, reminding the dark skies above us just how good and strong and loving and merciful our God is. We still our hearts and soak in the presence of God. And if we don't have money for food, we fast. Every trial and every problem can become an opportunity to grow closer to God.

Sometimes after we've been praying and waiting and resting with God, things get a little wild. We remember that God is still on the throne, being praised by the angels and strange-looking beasts and everything else that we read about in the book of Revelation. And we join in. We jump and sing and run around the compound shaking our tambourines and hitting our drums, giving God the glory He deserves.

We do all these things and more. But we never get to the point where we stop trusting God. We're founded on hope—it's in our blood and in our name—and we choose always to look to Him. He is the only source of love and hope on which we can rely.

* * * * * * * * * * * * *

By the time 2013 came around, Pierre-Richard and I were Mama and Pappy to 30 children. Some were too young for school, like Pierre-Richardson and Vance, and some were in their twenties, like Julmis and Celicia. Others, like Ludmie, we didn't adopt but have loved as if they were our own children anyway. She was already an independent adult when we met her, but she chose to work and live with us. She could have moved out and found a job in the city, but like most families in Haiti, children are welcome to stay for as long as they want. There is no pressure to leave at any age. So like Wilner and Luckmane, Ludmie has chosen to stay. In a family as big as ours, everybody has a role to play. Everybody has purpose. Everybody is loved.

Though we have long since filled the bedrooms in the house that Bill built, we still get asked regularly to take in new children and adopt them. We don't always say yes to every child, but we do pray earnestly about each. If God moves us and we're aware of His blessing, we'll say yes. But only if we are sure.

Sometimes, though, the answer is obvious—like the night Jabetta arrived.

. . . .

At 5:00 a.m., I woke up to the sound of voices outside the compound. Someone was calling my name, but it was a voice I didn't recognize. There was something else mixed up with the sound—it reminded me of a wounded animal. Whatever it was, it did not sound well.

Pierre-Richard and I went out and saw a woman our age clutching a pile of rags to her chest. I recognized the woman. We called her Matron, and she worked as a midwife in town. "Look," she said when she saw us. She eased the bundle away from her body so we could see. Inside was one of the smallest babies I'd ever seen. And it was in distress. Though the baby was fighting for breath, it was a losing battle.

We brought them both inside immediately, and as soon as we sat down, Matron told the story.

"A week ago, I was called out to visit a pregnant woman nearby. She had been keeping it a secret, especially from her husband, who is not the father. She was upset and said that she didn't want to be pregnant anymore. I told her that she had some more months left before the baby was ready to be born, perhaps two or three."

The baby cried some more, and Matron broke off her story to comfort her.

"The mother's sister came and found me tonight and told me that she had been drinking teas and taking pills to induce the baby. I got there as soon as I could. She had the crying baby on the floor." Matron was barely whispering as she carried on. "The mother was trying to strangle it with the cord. I pushed her away and cut the cord. Then I tried to give her the baby to feed, but she pushed me away and shouted that it wasn't her baby."

Even before Pierre-Richard spoke, I knew what he was going to say. Ever since Pierre-Richardson had come to live with us as a baby, Pierre-Richard had wanted a baby daughter. He loved all our children with such warmth and depth, but we both knew that there was a space in his heart for a little baby girl of his own.

"The baby," he said. "Is it a girl?"

Matron nodded. "Yes. But she's dying. She needs to get to a hospital right now. Will you take her?"

Even before the question had left her lips, Pierre-Richard and I were on our feet, ready to go. I scooped the baby up and followed Pierre-Richard to the car. She was so light and small that she could fit in my hand. I guessed she didn't weigh more than a pound and a few ounces. I held her close as Pierre-Richard drove us down the road, trying to cushion her against the jolts and bumps.

I had never been a pediatric nurse, but it was obvious that Matron was right. The little baby was struggling to breathe and was becoming increasingly distressed. Being born two or three months early, her lungs had not matured, and she needed a ventilator.

The doctor in the first hospital on the outskirts of Port-au-Prince took one look at her and shook his head. "I can't help. She's too weak and small. No baby that size ever makes it."

"No!" I said, far louder than I intended. "That's not okay. You need to treat her. We have money."

He raised his eyes and shook his head again. "There's no point. She's not going to make it. We've got a lot of sick babies and we have to prioritize the ones who can survive." He paused and shrugged. "Sorry."

I wanted to shout and scream, but I felt Pierre-Richard's hand on my shoulder. "It's okay," he said to me. He looked at the doctor and smiled. "Isn't there anything you can do? Please?"

He looked at the baby again. "Well…she's weak, so I suppose I could give you some dextrose."

Pierre-Richard uttered a quick "thank you" before I could say anything, and once we'd gotten the sugar syrup, we raced out to the car again.

The next hospital visit was even shorter. We were turned away at the door by a nurse. It was the same story in the next one as well. And the next.

By now it was nearly midday, and whatever benefit the baby was getting from the dextrose was fading. Her breathing grew irregular. She was running out of time, and we were almost out of hospitals.

There was one place left to visit, the worst hospital in all of Port-au-Prince.

It was the last place I wanted to take her. Everybody knew that it was filthy, and the few doctors and nurses they had were only there because they could not get a job at a better hospital. It was the sort that only occasionally paid its staff their wages. You had to buy gloves before they would even examine you. But we had no choice. No choice at all.

Even from outside, the smell was shocking. Inside, the walls were covered in filth of all kinds. Patients lay slumped on the floor. None of them looked like they were receiving any treatment. Some of them were barely breathing.

We found a nurse who peeled back the rags and stared. "I'll take her," she said, holding out her arms.

I was about to hand the baby over but stopped. "What will you do?"

"Do? There's nothing we can do. But we have a table where we put them when they're like this. Leave her with me. We'll deal with the body once she's dead."

I opened my mouth to shout but nothing came out.

"Ma'am, we don't even have space for babies that are born here. And this one isn't going to make it. You can see that she's in distress, can't you?"

Pierre-Richard stood up to leave, but I sat, rooted. Tears flooded my cheeks, and the baby's cries and mine blurred together.

"Sir?" Pierre-Richard was holding out his hand to an older man who was walking by. The man stopped, smiled, and wrapped Pierre-Richard up in a bear hug.

"What are you doing here, son?"

Pierre-Richard explained about the baby and got the man to take a look. "We just need someone to take her in and treat her. That's all."

The man smiled. "For you there is space." Then he called out to the nurse. "This is my son. Find space for his daughter."

The expression on the nurse's face changed instantly. She dropped her eyes, nodded, rushed back to the desk, and picked up the phone.

The man walked away, and I leaned over to Pierre-Richard. "Who is he?"

"The hospital administrator."

"Okay, but why does he call you his son?"

"He's a friend of my father's."

The nurse rushed back over and told us to follow her to a ward on the ground floor. She pointed to an incubator. "We can put the baby here, but you need to buy some things first. You need a bulb and sheet for the incubator, some latex gloves for the staff, and some meds. I'll get you the list."

I stayed with the baby while Pierre-Richard went and bought everything. It would have been quicker for us to split up and both go shopping, but I didn't trust the nurse completely. She was only helping because she wanted to impress her boss. I didn't feel like that was a solid enough reason for her to suddenly care whether the baby lived or died.

* * * * * * * * * * *

We stayed by the incubator all night and throughout the next day. Other babies were in the ward, and at least two of them died in the first few days that we were there. But the more time that passed, the stronger the baby's—our baby's—breathing became, and the calmer she grew.

She was a fighter. Every day we saw her determination to survive, and as we watched her—Pierre-Richard and I, as well as the visitors who came to see us—became convinced that God had a plan for this little girl's life.

Pierre-Richard and I both spent hours crying beside the incubator. At first the tears were of fear that this little life would slip away, but soon they flowed for a different reason. We wept because we were grateful—grateful that this tiny baby might just survive, grateful that God had yet again proven Himself to be faithful, grateful that the deepest desire of our hearts had been fulfilled.

All along, I'd held a concern in the back of my mind that the hospital was not a safe place for her. The lack of hygiene was obvious, and I wanted to get her out as soon as I could. When she was 15 days old and her oxygen level was at 70 percent, I felt the Lord say that it was time. "Time to take your child and go."

We returned home, stopping by the first hospital we had visited on the morning Matron had brought our baby to us. The same doctor saw us, and he was stunned. I asked him to test her oxygen levels, and he agreed.

"One hundred percent," he said, shaking his head and smiling. "That dextrose really worked, huh?"

Pierre-Richard and I drove the final few miles home in silence. My mind was feasting on a verse from Scripture:

> Jabez called upon the God of Israel, saying, "Oh that you would bless me and enlarge my border, and that your hand might be with me, and that you would keep me from harm so that it might not bring me pain!" And God granted what he asked (1 Chronicles 4:10).

The brief story of Jabez has been such an important part of Scripture for us. We have known pain and we have known God's protection and we have known His blessing. And this little baby, who was born in suffering, was in many ways the biggest blessing of all. She reminded us both that when God blesses, He blesses abundantly and in ways that perfectly demonstrate His goodness and love.

We prayed together. We talked. We sought permission from the family. And when that was done and the adoption papers were signed, we finally had a little baby girl of our own: Jabetta.

• • • • • • • • • • •

Neither Pierre-Richard nor I want our kids to start their day without knowing they've been in God's presence. We want them all to take a moment so that He can make Himself known to them for that day and give them their daily bread. Because of that, we sing.

A lot. We sing before we pray, and we sing before we sleep. We sing whenever we are driving in the bus, and we sing before we eat.

The words we sing are simple, but they are from the heart:

> *When I wake up in the morning the first thing I do*
> *—the first thing I long to do—*
> *Is to worship You.*
> *During the day and before I go to sleep*
> *I want to glorify You.*
> *A lot of great things that You have done in my life*
> *is nothing but favor.*
> *I bless Your name and I magnify Your name.*

We sing to remind ourselves that He is our comfort in times of sadness and our joy when times are good. We sing about the many ways He has saved us, and we sing about needing Him.

If we could only sing one song for the rest of our lives, it would be the one that we sing before every meal we eat in our house. We gather together, clapping and singing over and over until everyone has joined in: "Merci, Seigneur!"

* * * * * * * * * * * * *

One day when she was not quite three years old, Jabetta collapsed. I heard Pierre-Richard screaming at her to wake up, screaming at anyone to come and help. I ran and found him sitting on the ground behind our house, her body limp in his lap.

I tried to revive her, but nothing worked. For the second time in her short life, we ran to the car with her in our arms. Only this time it was so much worse. No crying. No struggles for breath. Just silence. I gave her mouth-to-mouth resuscitation as Pierre-Richard drove us to the doctor in town.

Again, we heard the same words: "There's nothing we can do."

Jabetta twitched, tensed up, and then exhaled. Pierre-Richard was weeping and I let out the biggest scream—"No!"

I was shouting at death, raging against it, trying with everything I had to force it back.

And then God stepped in.

A strange kind of calm settled on me—focused and determined, no longer frantic. She was God's child. She was safe in His arms.

Out of nowhere I had a sense that I needed to put my finger in her mouth and check yet again to see whether her airways were blocked. I did, and her little jaw was already beginning to seize up, like death was setting in. I found nothing, but as soon as I took my finger out, she gasped, inhaled deeply, and started breathing again.

She opened her eyes, looked at Pierre-Richard, and shouted, "Pappy!"

Later that day we took her to a new hospital, staffed by American and French doctors, and we heard that it had a working MRI scanner. They took Jabetta in—who was now smiling and giggling at anyone and anything—and checked her out.

The doctor came to see us in the waiting area.

"We couldn't find anything wrong at all," he said, inviting us back to see her.

We were still outside the ward when we heard her. She was singing at the top of her voice, calling out the words with the force of a hurricane:

"Merci Seigneur! Merci Seigneur! Merci Seigneur! Merci, merci Seigneur! Merci, merci Seigneur!"

18

SWEAT EQUITY

The first time I received a letter telling me I had won an award, I ignored it. I didn't feel like much of an award winner that day. We had no food at home, and my kids were hungry. What kind of mother gets a medal for having empty cupboards and growling tummies?

The second time they wrote to me, I ignored it again, but for different reasons. God had come through, like He always does, and we were no longer hungry. But how could I accept an award that had my name on it when there were so many others who had been involved and walked this journey with us?

The third time, however, I decided to talk to Pastor Jean about it.

"William Jefferson Clinton, as in President Clinton?"

"Yes," I said, "but it's not what you think. I'm just doing what God has called me to do, and I'm enjoying it. Why should I need an award for that?"

Pastor Jean read the e-mail again. "They say you do deserve it. You say you don't. You're probably right. But it doesn't have to be about you. Remember *sweat equity?*"

I smiled. It was a phrase he often used when he preached at church. He and I, plus all the people involved in Hope House Haiti and Hope Christian Academy, are all in the same position. We are not economically rich, but we can work. We can run the schools that offer education to children who cannot afford the high fees at almost every other school in the country. We can take those day-long journeys into the mountains to build relationships with communities. We can load our bus with food and water and visit the people whose poverty has made them vulnerable to the latest hurricane or flooding to hit the island. Hard work, commitment, and sweat are what we can bring to the table. That's our equity. We trust God to bring in people who will partner with us and provide what we lack—the money.

In the end, I took a flight to Dublin, Ireland with Pierre-Richard. It was a wonderful night celebrating the many ways that God is at work in Haiti. And when I walked up to the stage and held out my hand, I knew that I was accepting the award on behalf of the many people who have supported us: from Pierre-Richard and Marie to my sister Idoxie and brothers Pastor Jean and Telfort and their wives. From the church and villagers in Bolney, England to the churches and people of Nantucket and Charlotte. The teams from Haven, Ireland and Atlanta, Georgia. Even the young voodoo priest in Fond Parisien played his part, giving us food when we needed it.

God invites everyone to say yes to Him and come into His kingdom—*everyone.*

. . . .

For Pierre-Richard, myself, and all our family, saying yes to God means that we don't allow ourselves to be seduced by feeling comfortable. Of course, it's important that we're continually grateful to God for all the many, many blessings He has given us, but the last thing I want is for us to allow our comfort and security to insulate and isolate us from the needs of others. That's not always easy because isolation and insulation are exactly what comfort and security offer. But poverty, disaster, and suffering could visit us all at any time. None of us has a tight grip on life. We need to be on our knees for the people around us who are desperate and suffering. None of us is too young or too inexperienced, too poor or too old, to be compassionate.

That's why we started other schools. The school on our compound in Fond Parisien continues growing and has reached 1,000 pupils. We struggle each month to find the money to pay our teachers, yet in faith we have opened three other schools: one in the mountains, one in south, and another up north, just outside the town of Gros Morne.

If we were a business, none of this would make sense. We'd be overextended and undercapitalized, and our budgets would look unrealistic and laughable. But we're not a business. We're a family. And families are motivated by love, not profit. Sweat is our main equity. Compassion is our growth strategy. Prayer is our decision-making tool.

So when we woke up one day to the news that there had been an earthquake off the north coast of Haiti that had killed people in Gros Morne, we prayed. The next day, long before the sun rose, we loaded the bus and drove up to help.

Less than 48 hours after the earthquake killed 14 people, life had almost returned to normal—almost. What passes for normal in Haiti is often shocking for those who visit. Most of the rubble had been cleared, and several roadblocks had been set up. Streets that on any other day would be filled with cars and donkeys pulling carts were occupied by faded tents and tarps as hundreds of people chose to sleep under canvas instead of risk staying inside a building.

Haitians are a loud people. Car stereos and church speakers are always pushed so loud the speakers strain and crack with distortion. When Haitians talk, even our most boring of conversations can reach the volume of an argument. But when the last of the town's funerals took place beneath the heat of the late Tuesday morning sun, people stood in perfect silence as the white coffin was laid down and the lid peeled open. A boy young enough for his father to lift his coffin alone from the back of the car was being buried. There were no cries, no sobs—just silence.

The buildings were like the people. We had to look hard to find the story of the earthquake's impact. Some looked as though they were untouched, but on other streets as many as one in three houses had wide cracks that snaked down supporting pillars or stretched across doorways. From the outside, it didn't look too bad. But appearances can be deceiving.

We met Gideon Fresnel sitting outside his home. "We were inside when the first earthquake hit on Saturday night," he said. Along with his sister and two young daughters, he had run outside. There he saw the deep crack open up across the front of his single story home. He was worried but decided to take a risk and sleep inside that night. On Sunday night it was different. When the earth shook for a second time, a main supporting wall collapsed. They ran through dust and falling rubble. Instantly, their house became uninhabitable, their home a place of fear.

Gideon didn't feel safe sleeping on the streets. He was scared that leaving his home or garden unoccupied would invite thieves. He struggled to set up a shelter in his garden using an old piece of canvas and a rusty tent frame. The wind and the rain pounded them from the sides, and their neighbor's two-story building stared down at them, deep cracks along its walls. Another aftershock and Gideon's whole garden could be buried under a ton of brick.

I stepped out of Gideon's shelter and onto the street. A neighbor grabbed me, pulling me down an alley to see her home. She told me her name was Madame Anora and she was too old to run, so when the earthquake hit and the powdery mortar walls peeled away in chunks, she got to her knees and prayed. "I prayed that God would save us," she said. "I am still praying."

Like Gideon's family, Madame Anora and her children and grandchildren were too scared to sleep inside. Rebuilding was the only option for them. But like everyone, she knew that rebuilding was a fantasy. The government wouldn't help. They'd come eventually and tell people which houses must be abandoned and which ones could be repaired, but that would be all.

Nobody expected any of the major nonprofits to visit, either. Compared to the 2010 earthquake, which claimed 300,000 lives, Gros Morne simply wasn't bad enough. For a town of 7,000, that would mean that hundreds—perhaps even thousands—of residents would be left permanently homeless, with zero support.

"Everyone has problems," said Gideon when he saw me on the street again. "Nobody will help us."

I knew he was right. I felt hopeless and helpless as I stood there. I wanted to tell him that I could rebuild his home, but we barely had enough money for gas to get back to Fond Parisien. The last thing I wanted to give him was false hope.

But I also knew that Gideon was wrong. He was not alone. People do care. God had sent help. "I will do what I can," I said. "We'll come back and help you build a better tent."

All we have is sweat equity and prayer, but it would be enough to help just one person, one family at a time. And then we would ask God to lead us to help another. And another. That is all we're called to do.

The day after we returned from Gros Morne, I stepped out of my bedroom and joined the girls who had gathered and started to worship. It was before six, and the boys were yet to join us. The girls and I exchanged smiles. I knew they remembered what I have said to them so often on other mornings. "Don't worry if the boys are late. When Jesus rose from the dead, who was waiting for Him in the garden? That's right, the women!"

We sang songs with words and melodies as familiar to us as the creases on our palms. As the rest of the family drifted in and the volume grew louder, I thought about Gideon and Madame Anora. I thought about the fact that so many Christians spend a lot of time worrying about their calling, as if God hides it, shrouding it in mystery. But God's calling is not hard to determine. God's calling is clear: He calls us to be partners with Him. He calls us to resist being lukewarm. He calls us to surrender ourselves so that the things that break His heart will also break ours.

It can be tempting to try to do things on our own. I did, and I never saw any real fruit. When we were working in Fonds Baillard, kids were being healed. They were learning and getting fed and getting clean—so something good was happening—but it took the earthquake to make me see the bigger picture. I finally understood that when I said yes to partnering with God, I was also saying yes to partnering with His people. Those people brought in what Pierre-Richard and I did not have. They brought what God had given them to bring—knowledge, friendship, encouragement, and love. These were the things that we needed, though many times we didn't know it ourselves.

If this book has a purpose, it is not that more people would know my name or even be aware of the work going on in Haiti. The purpose is so much bigger. I hope that as you reach these final pages, you know that God is alive. I hope you know that He heals, He transforms, and He speaks to people today. And if you know that, I hope you have caught hold of the idea that when God speaks, something wonderful happens to those who obey. They get to know Him better.

This is not a new idea. Read the Bible and you will see the same God working in the same way, inviting the same kind of people to join Him. Like us, they're flawed, broken, and so often get things wrong. But nothing is too much for God.

We see it in Abraham's life and we see it in Moses's life. Esther takes a risk and says yes to God's plan, just like Noah and so many others. God calls us to be His friend, to trust Him, to partner with Him, to work with Him.

. . . .

We ended our time of singing and prayer the morning after the Gros Morne visit in the same way that we finish every one of these times. We hugged, smiled, and laughed. In the few minutes before it was time to get ready for school, there was a pause. I looked around at my family. Junior wanted to show some of his brothers a new trick he'd learned with a soccer ball. Lorina had a math problem that she needed help with, and only Fabian would do. Jabetta was standing, hands on hips, telling off her brothers that were twice as tall as her for not asking when they borrowed her pencils.

Twenty-one boys, 17 girls, and a handful of adults like Pierre-Richard's mom and my brothers and their wives. That's a lot of people. But it's not a crowd. It's my family. We laugh and joke and fight like any other family. We go to the lake on special days and swim in the water, laughing at Pappy's jokes. We give thanks when we remind each other of all the good things God has done for us, and we cry together when times are tough.

My prayer for each of my children is the same as my prayer for you. May you look back on all that God has done and be drawn to know Him more. May these stories of God's faithfulness, love, and kindness awaken deep within you a hunger for Him. And as you close these pages and set this book down, may you say yes to God. And as you do, may you become the mama or the pappy, the pastor or the teacher, the defender or the friend that He created you to be.

ABOUT THE AUTHOR

Yvrose Telfort Ismael is a William Jefferson Clinton Goodwill for Haiti award recipient. She is known as Mammy to 38 children born of her heart. She and her husband, Pierre-Richard, cofounded Hope House, the children's home they established in the aftermath of Haiti's 2010 catastrophic earthquake. The two also run a free school serving underprivileged children in their community.

Craig Borlase is a *New York Times* bestselling author, specializing in crafting dramatic, engaging memoirs. He has collaborated with a wide range of people, including a two-time Grammy winning songwriter, an Iranian refugee who spent four months in a Turkish jail, a female transatlantic rower, a World War II veteran, and a former Muslim woman who was one week away from becoming a suicide bomber.

His most recent collaboration is *Finding Gobi*, the *New York Times* bestselling account of an ultramarathon runner's chance encounter with a stray dog in the Mongolian desert. Previous work has taken him to Iraq, Jordan, China, Cuba, Uganda, Australia, and all over the United States.

To learn more about Harvest House books and
to read sample chapters, visit our website:

www.harvesthousepublishers.com

HARVEST HOUSE PUBLISHERS
EUGENE, OREGON